Piero Torriti
Superintendent to the Artistic and
Historical Assets of the Provinces of
Siena and Grosseto

ALL SIENA

THE CONTRADE AND THE PALIO

344 COLOUR ILLUSTRATIONS

MAP OF THE TOWN

BONECHI - EDIZIONI «IL TURISMO» - FLORENCE

Photographic sources: *Photographic Archives of the Soprinten-denza ai Beni Artistici e Storici per le Province di Siena e Grosseto; Municipality of Siena; Monte dei Paschi di Siena; Azienda Autonoma per il Turismo di Siena; Istituto Fotografico Editoriale Scala di Firenze; Foto Grassi di Siena; Archives of Bonechi Edizioni; Paolo Torriti; Rolando Fusi; Studio Gielle, Siena.*

Diagrams: *on page 22 from E. Carli - A. Cairola - «Il Palazzo Pubblico di Siena», Rome 1963; on page 30 from E. Carli - «Il Duomo di Siena», Genoa 1979; on page 115 from «Guida al Palio di Siena», Monte dei Paschi Editions, 1986.*

Road map: *Bonechi - Edizioni «Il Turismo» S.r.l.*

Lay-out: *Piero Bonechi - Rolando Fusi*
Coordination: *Simonetta Giorgi*
Translation: *Rosalynd Pio*
Typesetting: *Leadercomp - Florence*
Colour separation: *La Fotolitografia - Florence*

Night view of Siena.

HISTORICAL OUTLINE

Siena was founded in the reign of Octavian Augustus, by the Romans, who built a military colony (Saena Julia) on the site of a preexisting Etruscan and perhaps Gaulish (the Saenones) settlement. The Roman origins of the town explain the heraldic charge the Medieval town chose for itself (the She-wolf feeding Romulus and Remus), which, together with the argent and sable coat divided per fess (la Balzana) were used by the town as its arms. Roman Siena was never very important, chiefly because it did not lie on any of the main consular roads (Aurelia and Cassia), which originally wound along the coast and along the Chiana Valley. For the same reasons, Christianity only reached Sienese territory towards the beginnings of the IVth cent. After the first Barbarian invasions had swept through Italy and after the Byzantine-Gothic war, Siena became part of the Longobard dominions. The Longobards settled in Siena and promoted the expansion of the Sienese territory to the detriment of nearby Arezzo. The road network shifted its axis and the Aurelia and the Cassia, which drove through areas exposed to the Byzantine inroads, were gradually abandoned to the advantage of the Via Francigena, that linked the Northern Longobard possessions with Rome, passing through Siena. In 774, the Longobards were conquered by Charlemagne and Siena was overrun by Frankish administrators,

who married into the Longobard families, originating the oldest aristocratic families in Siena and founding abbeys and castles all over the Sienese territory. Feudal power gradually decreased and at the death of the Countess Matilda (1115), the Mark of Tuscia, which under the Canossa family (Matilda's) included most of Tuscany as it is today, broke up into a series of burgeoning communal structures. The Commune of Siena, with its territory bordering dangerously on Guelphish Florence, a traditional enemy of Siena, declared its allegiance to the Ghibelline cause. Between the 12th and 13th centuries, the ancient Early-Medieval «civitas» of Siena expanded to join the two boroughs or agglomerations of houses that had grown up along the Via Francigena, to the North and East of the town, thus originating the three «thirds» (terzi) of Città, Camollia and San Martino. Money-lending and exchange activities gave the town great prosperity, as they led the citizens to ply their trade all over Europe (Champagne, Flanders and England). Towards the beginning of the 13th century, the consular regime was replaced by the Podestà system and Siena became one of the most active Tuscan partisans of Frederick II's successor, Manfred of Swabia, King of Sicily. The war against Florence reached its apex at the battle of Montaperti, when the Ghibelline Sienese army massacred the Guelph army of Florence (4th Sept. 1260). The regime of the Podestàs fell in Siena as it did in the Northern and Central Italian towns, when the burgher class started demanding that it should share the administrative power in the town together with the patricians. The regime of the Nine commenced in 1287 and lasted for about seventy relatively

Aerial view of Siena.

tranquil years. Its representatives were mostly rich burghers who were appointed in rotation every two months. This was the period during which the Salimbeni, Tolomei, Sansedoni, Buonsignori, Piccolomini and Gallerani families rose to power and innumerable great artists such as Duccio di Buoninsegna, Simone Martini, Ambrogio and Piero Lorenzetti, Niccolò and Giovanni Pisano, Tino da Camaino and many others graced Siena with their presence. These were the years when the construction of the Palazzo Pubblico was commenced, when the plans for enlarging the Cathedral (never completed) were drawn, when the last circle of the walls (still standing) was built. In 1348, Siena, like most of Europe, was hit by the terrible Black Death, which not only exterminated four fifths of the population, but destabilized the political scene. When the Government of the Nine was overthrown, in 1355, the so-called Monti, or groups of powerful patrician and burgher families took over the administration of the town. Caterina Benincasa (St. Catherine of Siena), a typical exponent of medieval religious Siena, lived throughout this period, and Bartolo di Fredi, Taddeo di Bartolo, Andrea di Bartolo, etc. emerged on the painting scene. During the 1390s, with a view to protecting herself from Florence, Siena placed herself under the Seigneury of Gian Galeazzo Visconti, Duke of Milan, but after his death (1404), the turbulent communal strife resumed. These were the years in which Sienese painting was represented by Sassetta, Vecchietta, Francesco di Giorgio Martini, and Sano di Pietro. The Renaissance emerged in Jacopo della Quercia's sculpture, while the humanist pope Pius II (Enea Silvio Piccolomini) promoted the activity on

Sienese soil of Florentine artists like Bernardo Rossellino. At the end of the 1400s, Siena had to accept the alliance with Charles V of Spain, who ordered a fortress built for the Spanish forces within the town, arousing violent popular reaction that led to the breaking of the alliance (1552) with the Emperor of Spain, who thereafter sought the friendship of Cosimo I de'Medici in Florence. Siena became an ally of France, but in the end, beleaguered by the Florentine and Spanish forces, was forced to capitulate in April 1555. Siena was handed over to Philip II, King of Spain who granted it in fief to Cosimo I de'Medici (who thus became Duke of Florence and Siena and subsequently – in 1569 – Grand Duke of Tuscany, thanks to the extension of the teritories under his sway). Under the Medici family, Siena clung to the memory of her erstwhile freedom and the factious spirit of her inhabitants, no longer allowed to participate in the political events of the city, was unleashed in passionate allegiance to the respective «contrade» of each native of Siena. The city maintained its independance in the artistic field, thanks to Domenico Beccafumi, Baldassarre Peruzzi and others. The banking tradition evolved from the private to the public status and the ancient Monte di Pietà, founded in 1472 became the Monte dei Paschi in 1624. After the advent of the Hapsburg-Lorraine family (1737), the last vestiges of the Republic disappeared and the town became an integral part of the Grand-duchy of Tuscany. The town's marked individuality is however apparent today in the attachment each Sienese feels towards his or her contrada and in the passionate involvement in the Palio, the most evident example of the exuberant nature of Siena's citizens.

Above: **Piazza del Campo, by Giuseppe Zocchi** (Monte dei Paschi Coll.) *below*: **aerial view of Piazza del Campo.**

PIAZZA DEL CAMPO

Over the centuries, the different styles which have grown into each other in the various patrician mansions arranged around the Piazza del Campo have produced an overall harmony, making it one of the most fascinating main squares in Europe. The middle of the square is paved with hand-made bricks, laid edgeways in a fish-bone pattern, and divided by nine strips of travertine that branch out from the shell shaped drain at the lowest point of the concave slope of the square – in honour of the Government of the Nine Lords (i Signori Nove) which presided over the town from 1285 to 1355. Nearly all the most important events in Siena's history

Piazza del Campo from the Mangia Tower.

Above: the ancient Fonte Gaia in a photograph taken during the last century; *below*: the new Fonte Gaia, by Tito Sarrocchi.

have taken place in or around this square. Some of them were auspicious – other less so; some took place during the era of the Republic (before 1555), others after the town became a dominion of Florence. The most deeply-felt event is the Palio that takes place here every year on the 2nd July and on the 16th August, making the heart of every Sienese throb in agonizing anticipation. Even today, the history of Siena and of its people cannot be recounted without mentioning the «contrade» and the Palio, which is no spontaneous, joyous folklore celebration or popular tradition, but the ultimate synthesis of the Sienese lifestyle: at all times and on public or private levels, the people of Siena re-enact and merge past and present in the activity of their *contrada* (the local name of the districts of Siena) – maintaining a kind of admirable and surprising continuity, a kind of minute republican democracy, which is that much more real than the ones «outside».

FONTE GAIA

In order to channel water from distant Staggia to Piazza del Campo, Giacomo di Vanni di Ugolino (later called Giacomo dell'Acqua) spent about eight years mainly digging great underground canals (today called the *Bottini* – or conduits) which, as they approached the town precincts, widened into brick-lined galleries of exceptional technical and artistic interest. Charles V, after visiting the Sienese «bottini», is supposed to have exclaimed that Siena was two cities in one, each as beautiful as the other, the first underground, the second above. Water was conveyed to Piazza del Campo through a Master-conduit, most likely first utilized around 1342. «The Sienese saluted the event with great rejoicing», wherefore the fountain, appropriately named Fonte Gaia (Gay Fountain), was built the following year (1343).The 14th century Fonte Gaia, about which we have practically no information, was replaced in 1419 by Jacopo della Quercia's and then by Tito Sarrocchi's free adaptation

Detail of the new Fonte Gaia.

The Chapel on Piazza del Campo.

of it in 1858. The two statues of Rea Silvia and Acca Lorenzia, that Jacopo had placed at each end of his fountain, were omitted from Sarrocchi's copy. The original marble statues by Jacopo della Quercia are now arranged along the back wall of the Loggia of Palazzo Pubblico, overlooking the Market square. Although its present state is decidedly lamentable, Jacopo's Fonte Gaia is still one of the most important works of the Italian 15th century and an example of the Gothic-Renaissance transition period. The *Madonna and Child*, a symbol taken from Lorenzetti's Allegory of Good Government, is flanked by two angels, the *Theological and Cardinal Virtues* and by *Justice*. Successive changes in the project led Jacopo to add the statues of the *Expulsion from Paradise*, the *Creation of Adam* as well as the two statues of *Acca Larentia* and *Rea Silvia* (respectively mother and nurse of Romulus and Remus): the first two female nudes to stand in a public place, who were neither Eve nor the Magdalen.

CHAPEL OF PIAZZA DEL CAMPO

Because of a solemn vow made during the terrible plague of 1348, the Commune of Siena commissioned the Cappella di Piazza (Chapel on the Square) which sticks out at the foot of the Mangia Tower. At first, Domenico di Agostino, then overseer at the Opera del Duomo (Cathedral Works) and brother to the better known Giovanni, was put in charge of the project. The four corner piers, called «more», were built somewhat later, in 1376 by Giovanni di Cecco. A plain roof covered the piers until Antonio Federighi replaced it during the Renaissance (1461-1468) with a vaulted roof, supported by rounded arches, with niches in the corners, garlands adorning the pendentives and a purely classical architrave decorated with a frieze of gryphons and vases. The *side-balustrades* are two

13th century marble panels, which are thought to have come from the ancient Baptisimal Font in the Cathedral. The two figures of *Arithmetic* and *Geometry*, on the front panels, were sculpted by Guidoccio Cozzarelli (1470). In 1848, they were replaced by copies carved by Enea Becheroni while the Cozzarelli originals were hung inside the Palace on the walls of the main staircase. The elegant *grilles* in beaten iron on either side of the Chapel were made in the second half of the 14th century. They probably belonged to the first Chapel of the Nine, on the ground floor of the Palazzo Pubblico, and were forged by Pietro di Betto, helped, according to some accounts, by Conte di Lello Orlandi, another Sienese ironworker. To the left of the altar, behind a small ancient beaten iron grille, there is a stone shrine, with an *Annunciation* and a *Christ Blessing* on the tympanum, by an unknown Sienese carver of the late 14th century. The fresco above the altar, is almost indescipherable. It was painted by Sodoma between 1537 and 1539.

7

PALAZZO PUBBLICO

It is thought that the first nucleus was a low, one-storey construction with a simple stone façade, having four openings leading into a large hall and a courtyard, which was finished around 1284 as the chronicles of that year, by Paolo Tommaso Montauri, relate. In 1288, however, the Council decided to construct a new palace at the bottom of the Campo. A few years later, the construction of the central part of the palace was commenced. It was not unlike the building we see today: the stone-dressed ground-floor with its four ogival openings; the first brick storey with four triple-mullioned windows and the second storey, also in brick, which probably had five triple-mullioned windows to start with, later reduced to four, for the sake of uniformity, while the two second floor wings were added in 1680, in the Baroque period. Around 1310. the building was probably already finished, as the Government of the Nine adopted it as their headquarters in that year. The nine inmates of the Palace were never allowed out of it except on feast-days. The ground-floor façade was given ten open door-ways, of which the fourth from the right of anyone looking at the building, led into the so-called Chapel of the Nine, frescoed by 14th century painters. After the fairly drastic restoration carried out throughout the late 1890s and the early 1900s, the façade has taken on a plain, fairly undecorated appearance. The architectural elements soar vertically upwards, only interrupted by the great openings of the twin and triple mullioned windows and countering all sense of massive strength with the frail elegance of the façade's delicate linearism. The *Siena arms* or *Balzana* (argent and sable party per fess) are set into the ogival arch of each window, whilst the great *Monogramme of St. Bernardino* (a flaming sun-disk inscribed with the monogramme of Christ) replaces the original central twin mullioned window on the third storey level. The *Medici arms* were added in 1560 to commemorate the annexation of Siena to the

Above and opposite: **two views of Palazzo Pubblico.**

grand-duchy of Tuscany. The Medici crest is flanked by the *Balzana* and by the people's *Lion Rampant*. Two stone *she-wolf-shaped gargoyles* stick out on each side of the central block. The main-entrance tympanum has the *Lion of the people* in the centre, flanked by two *She-wolves* in relief while a stat-uette of *St. Ansanus* stands above the tympanum. At one end of the façade, near the main entrance, there used to be a granite column bearing the gilded bronze *she-wolf with the Roman twins*, cast by Giovanni and Lorenzo di Turino in 1430. The she-wolf feeding Romulus and Remus is the symbol of Siena. The mythical brothers, Aschius and Senius, sons of Remus, are supposed to have fled from the wrath of Romulus, bearing an effigy of the Roman She-wolf, as a symbol of their lost home-land, with them. They reputedly took refuge in the Tuscan hills, where Senius later founded the town (Senius: Sena – Siena).

Detail of the Mangia Tower.

The **Mangia Tower**, which derives its name from Giovanni di Balduccio or Duccio, who was nicknamed Mangiaguadagni (literally Earnings-gobbler) or Mangia (Gobbler), who used to be the bellman before a mechanism was installed to replace him, lends the whole complex of the Palazzo Pubblico its extraordinarily delicate, vertically-oriented elegance. It was started in 1325 and finished in 1348. It was intended as a symbol of the power of the palace inmates and of the town itself. The tower is 87 ms. high (102 ms., if one includes the lightening conductor). The brothers Francesco and Muccio (or Minuccio) di Rinaldo from Arezzo were given the technical responsibility of the construction (1338-40) and they therefore shouldered the risks and expense of the building operations. The tower is entirely in brick, up to the soaring white travertine pronged supports of the bell-chamber balustrade, which give the whole tower the appearance of a tall slender lily. the latter part was probably built by Agostino di Giovanni, based on the designs of a certain 'Master Lippo – painter', almost certainly to be identified as the great Lippo Memmi, brother in law to Simone Martini (1341. The present master bell (called «Campanone», or «Sunto») weighs 6764 kgs. and was hung in 1666.

INTERIOR OF PALAZZO PUBBLICO

There are, at present, two entries to the Town Hall on the Piazza. The first, through the two doors to the left, next to the Chapel, leads into the Courtyard of the Podestà, where, amidst the many *family crests* of the governors, the remains of the stone statue of *Mangia* are preserved. At the end of the courtyard, steps lead up to the **Teatro dei Rinnovati**, ex Great Council Chamber of the Republic. A side door opens onto a modern hanging staircase leading down to a whole series of lovely, semi-underground halls, with brick vaults, erstwhile cisterns and store-rooms of the Palace («**Magazzini del Sale**» or «Salt Deposits»), which have been beautifully restored and are now used for temporary exhibitions. Some of the rooms contain the *Quadreria* or *Picture Gallery* of various schools and periods,

View of Siena in a painting by Sano di Pietro (National Picture Gallery).

Above: **the courtyard of Palazzo Pubblico**; *below*: **the Meeting at Teano, by Pietro Aldi** (Risorgimento Hall).

mostly moved here from the old Civic Museum. The marble *Sienese She-wolf* (1487) which used to stand on the column in Piazza Postierla, which still marks the Terziere di Città (the third of the town – terziere – occupying the site of the original Roman settlement), has recently been placed on the hanging staircase. The small room leading to the entrance to the Mangia Tower, also leads into the **Hall of the Risorgimento** (ex-Audience Hall of the Podestà) where a large number of 19th century pieces of *sculpture* and *paintings* have been arranged.

The other door, on the right, opens into a long passage, leading to a steep staircase, which climbs up to the Loggia of the Fonte Gaia and the upper floor. Next to the door leading into the

passage, one enters the so-called **Sala di Balìa** (Hall of the Bailies), where the Bailie (the representatives of the executive power of the Republic – generally eight citizens (bailies), granted extensive powers, foregathered as from 1455. The hall is completely frescoed in Late-Gothic style by a Sienese (Martino di Bartolomeo) and by a citizen of Arezzo, who had learnt his craft in Florence: Spinello Aretino, who was, in fact, called after his home-town). The former painted the *Virtues* in the vault sections and on the pillars and the four *Evangelists* on the intrados of the great arch that divides the hall into two sections, as well as six busts of *emperors* and *warriors*, including, they say, Godfrey of Bouillon, on the piers and pendentives of the arch itself. In 1408, Spinello Aretino was given the more complicated task of recording the deeds of Pope Alexander III a member of the Sienese Bandinelli family, the inspiring force behind the Lombard League and deadly enemy of Barbarossa (Frederick Redbeard) as well as probable promoter of the foundation of the Cathedral of Siena. The beautiful inlaid *door*, (1426) which leads into the **Inner Chapel**, is attributed to Domenico di Niccolò (called «dei Cori» because he also made the wonderful intaglioed and inlaid choir stalls of this palace chapel). The magnificent *choir stalls* flanking the altar were carved by Domenico di Niccolò between 1514 and 1428. There are 21 stalls, each decorated with a scene illustrating some *article of the Creed*. Also by Domenico, the splendid left door frame decorated with a *Nativity* scene and a *Wheel* – symbolizing the allegories of good and bad power. The vaults and walls of the chapel are all frescoed by the late-Gothic Sienese painter, Taddeo di Bartolo, with five *Stories from the Life of the Virgin*. Taddeo di Bartolo also painted the colossal *St. Christopher* (1408) and a cycle of political Virtues and illustrious men (1414) in the *Antichapel*; the cycle quite obviously refers to the ideas and lifestyle of the Sienese republic in the early 15th century. There are five Virtues illustrated (*Fortitude, Prudence, Faith, Justice and Magnanimity*), surrounded by the portraits of illustrious personalities of ancient Rome (*Cato, Brutus, Mutius Scaevola, Attilius Regulus, Scipio*, ect.). The intrados of

Above: **Sala di Balìa** (Hall of the Bailies); *below*: the **Dormitio Virginis**, by Taddeo di Bartolo (Inner Chapel).

Above: **the Inner Chapel;** *below*: **Holy Family, by Sodoma; Wooden Lamp and detail from an inlaid panel, by Domenico di Niccolò dei Cori** (Inner Chapel).

Above: **the Maestà (Madonna and Child enthroned), by Simone Martini**; *below*: **the Map Hall.**

the great arch, on the Sala del Mappamondo (Map Hall) side, is decorated with a view of Rome, surrounded by the figures of *Jupiter, Mars, Apollo, Pallas Athene, Aristotle, Caesar* and *Pompey*. In 1959, the gilded bronze *She-wolf, feeding the twins* was placed in the vestibule. The statue was cast in 1429 by Giovanni di Turino and his son Lorenzo and was placed on the column in front of the Palazzo Pubblico. Antonio Bazzi, called Sodoma, painted the panel above the Chapel Altar. It shows the *Holy Family with St. Leonard* and is one of his most significant works (dated 1530-35). Sodoma was a pupil of Leonardo and came from Vercelli. A carved and gilded wooden *lamp* hangs from the chapel vault. It is a rare piece, the intaglio work of which has been recognized as being by Domenico di Niccolò dei Cori, and is dated just before 1435. Next to the chapel is the great hall, called **Sala del Mappamondo** (Map Hall), where the Council of the Republic met. The end-wall is covered by Simone Martini's magnificent **Maestà** (1315 and 1321), one of the greatest European Gothic masterpieces. The novel, significant conceptions this work expresses, compared for instance, with the other famous *Maestà* by Duccio di Buoninsegna in the Cathedral Museum (Museo dell'Opera del Duomo) are a perfect definition of the new courtly ideals of the 14th century, which blossom in the pages of Petrarch's Canzoniere (Petrarch was a friend of Simone) or in the tales of Boccaccio's Decameron. Simone's frescoed Virgin no longer conforms to the strict canons of Byzantine iconography, as Duccio's Madonna does in his gigantic panel. She is a more human «Mater», who has graciously stepped-down to honour the people of Siena, while two angels offer cups brimming over with flowers, as she sits among her blessed heavenly courtiers. These were new emotions compared with the early Middle Ages and it is the compositional aspect that is more truly revolutionary than the figures and subject chosen. The harmonious lines flowing almost uninterruptedly from one figure to the other, the tenuous, transparent colours, the ample drapery, the movement of the canopy, the swaying grace of the figures, specially the kneeling ones, the rich embroidery and the

Detail from the Maestà, by Simone Martini (Map Hall).

gleaming golden haloes and throne do away with the hieratic quality of the Byzantine heritage which we still perceive in Duccio's *Maestà* (which predates Simone's by a bare four years) and is to be observed in all previous painting. The top of the end wall opposite the Maestà is frescoed with the *1328 Siege of the Castle of Montemassi in Maremma* conducted by **Guido Riccio da Fogliano**, then captain of the

Sienese army. The name of Simone Martini is linked to this world-famous fresco as well. It has become the symbol of the civilian and military glory of the ancient Republic of Siena and is a kind of counterchant to the religious glory epitomised by the courtly language used in the Maestà on the opposite wall. The knight in his surcoat embroidered with the device of the Da Fogliano family (twining vine tendrils

Above: **the She-wolf, by Giovanni di Turino;** *below*: **detail from Guido Riccio da Fogliano, by Simone Martini.**

sprouting from a line of dark blue lozenges on golden ground) rides a horse caparisoned with the same device. Although the features of the knight are portrayed with due attention, the central group appears to possess no physical solidity whatsoever, as if the modulated construction were an abstract symphony of pure musical chords, rung out by the flowing line of lozenges on the caparisoned horse and on the knight's surcoat, the whole set-off by the instable equilibrium of the horse, who seems to be floating in mid-air. This unreal metaphysical quality enhances the magic of the scene, its apparition-like sense is also to be perceived in the background, where the castle of Montemassi, the keep with its turrets and catapult and the Sienese army encampment stand etched out against the barren clay hills («crete») of the Maremma. Next to the Map Hall is the Hall of the Nine, better known as the **Hall of Peace**, thanks to an allegorical figure painted there. The frescoes, of great artistic and historical value, are world-famous. They cover three sides of the hall and represent the *Allegory of Good and Bad Government*, which the great Ambrogio Lorenzetti was commissioned to paint for the

Above: **Guido Riccio da Fogliano, by Simone Martini;** *below*: **the Hall of Peace.**

Above: **Allegory of Good Government, by Ambrogio Lorenzetti;** *below*: **two details from the same.**

Government of the Nine, between 1338 and 1340. The shorter wall opposite the great windows bears the Allegory of Good Government proper. It is sprinkled with innumerable inscriptions identifying the various figures and centres on the Common Weal. The usual she-wolf feeding the twins lies at his feet. The kingly old man is flanked by Peace, Fortitude, Prudence, Magnanimity, Temperance and Justice, while Faith, Hope and Charity hover around his head. Knights in armour stand guard, below right, over a group of prisoners or evil-doers. The slow cortège of the rulers conversing among themselves winds its way towards the old man, while the knights and prisoners add a note of deeper humanity to the magnificent composition. The ethical and political meanings which Simone Martini expressed in a totally different vein in the frescoes we have just described in the Map Hall, are reiterated in this Allegory by Ambrogio, far more punctually and in a less abstract fashion with the object of pointing out that a state can only be well-governed by the Virtues (with especial reference to Justice and Concord) which spontaneosly generate Safety, flying high above the red gateway of Siena, in the fresco on the right wall. Ambrogio's cycle (the first to be based on a profane or non-sacred theme in the history of painting, as many critics have observed) is at its very best on the right wall, where he lovingly describes the *Effects of Good Government on Siena and its territory*. The delightfully realistic details of the happy, well-governed city, inhabited by its contentedly laborious citizens engaged in their manifold activities both within and outside the walls are depicted in all their variety beneath the winged figure of Safety hovering above the russet tower-gate of Siena. For the first time in Italian history of art, the positive effects of good government on a state's citizens are expressed visually, without the mediation of symbolism: merchants stand at their counters in their shops opening onto the streets, schoolchildren toil at their letters, processions and children at play crowd the streets, farm workers happily harvest their crops against the timeless loveliness of the carefully tilled fields and vineyards of the Sienese countryside, returning serenely to their well-ordered

Above and below: **the figure of Peace and the Countryside in the Allegory of Good Government, by Ambrogio Lorenzetti.**

Left: **Madonna and Child enthroned, by Guido da Siena;** *above and below*: **details from the frescoes by D. Beccafumi (**Hall of the Concistory**).**

farmyards set among the eternally modern chromatic splendour of the patchworked Sienese hills that shed their tranquil beauty on the visitor to this renowned hall. On the opposite wall, where the effects of *Bad Government* were effigied, the composition has been disrupted by the disappearance of numerous portions of the fresco, mainly owing to wear and tear. The allegory

itself is centred on the figure of Tyranny enthroned. At his feet is a black billy-goat and he is flanked by the sinister figures of Cruelty, Deceit, Fraudulence, Fury, Discord and War. Avarice, Pride and Vainglory crowd around his head. The humiliated figure of Justice in chains crouches beneath his throne. The **Sala dei Pilastri** (Hall of the Pillars) contains a great panel of the *Madonna and*

Child; the Redeemer blessing in the cusp, flanked by two angels, one of the most significant paintings by the first known Sienese painter: Guido da Siena. An elegant Renaissance marble *doorway*, carved by Bernardo Rossellino in 1446, leads into the last hall on the left (the inlaid and intaglioed *doors* were carved by Domenico di Niccolò dei Cori in 1444). The hall is called **Sala del**

Above: **Judgement of Solomon, by Luca Giordano and overall view of the Hall of the Concistory;** *below*: **St. Bernardino preaching and the Miracle of the Possessed Woman, by Neroccio di Bartolommeo.**

Concistoro (Hall of the Concistory), or Hall of the Arras, because of the three magnificent Gobelin tapestries, woven to designs by Charles Le Brun (17th century) hanging on the walls. They represent the *Allegories of Earth, Air and Fire*. The great artistic importance of this hall is mainly due, however, to the superbly luminous frescoes that Domenico di Pace, called Beccafumi,

painted between 1529 and 1535 on the ceiling vaults. Like Ambrogio Lorenzetti before him, in the Hall of Peace, he depicted episodes of civic Virtue drawn from Valerius Maximus. Beccafumi's brilliant colours provide a sensation of cristalline purity and transparent delicacy and the clarity of the fresco's luminous tones, combined with the airy, beautifully executed perspective

are in perfect accord with the most refined Tuscan Mannerist dictates, to such an extent that the technical and pictorial ability employed lend the whole a vaguely cold and artificial sensation. There is an admirable painting by Luca Giordano (Naples 1634 1705) of the *Judgement of Solomon* above the doorway.

In the 14th century, splendid family

21

Left: detail of **Palazzo Sansedoni**; *above*: bird's eye-view of **Piazza del Campo**; *below*: plan of the square.

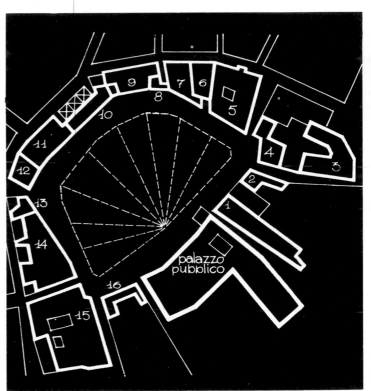

1. Palazzo Petroni
2. Palazzo Piccolomini Salamoneschi
3. Palazzo Piccolomini
4. Palazzo Ragnoni
5. Palazzo Mezolombardi Rinaldini
6. Palazzo Tornainpuglia Sansedoni
7. Palazzo Vincenti
8. Palazzo Piccolomini
9. Palazzo Rimbotti
10. Seat of the Merchants' Hall
11. Palazzo Saracini
12. Palazzo Scotti
13. Palazzo Accarigi
14. Palazzo Alessi
15. Palazzo Mattasala Lambertini
16. Casa Beringeri Antolini (?)

«Bocca di Casato», in Piazza del Campo.

Palazzo Chigi-Saracini, in via di Città.

mansions, nearly all in brick with twin or triple-mullioned windows surrounded the square, as a decree contained in the Statute of the Republic ordained. They were separated by the narrow alleys leading into the square itself. The diagram on page 22 shows who owned each mansion around the 14th century. Notwithstanding the massive restructuring, the medieval square's ancient harmony is still delightfully apparent. From Piazza del Campo, one has to climb up the incline of the *Costarella dei Barbieri* towards the Cathedral. This is where the horses starting and arrival post (la mossa) is, during the Palio race. Opposite, abutting onto Via di Città, is the tower mansion that used to be the seat of the Podestà (kind of governor) of Siena, which leads one on to the neighbouring *Palazzo Pollini*, that stands between the left corner of the

Costarella and the Via di Città, which, at this point starts ascending slowly towards the more ancient centre of the town. **Via di Città**, erstwhile Via Galgaria, is one of the loveliest and most elegant streets in Siena. It is lined with buildings constructed in various periods, starting from the 13th century, when numerous wooden houses were replaced by stone and brick buildings.

PALAZZO CHIGI-SARACINI

Further on, on the left, at number 89, one encounters Palazzo Chigi Saracini, a stone building decorated in brick; the original nucleus of the house belonged

to the Marescotti family, who throughout the 14th century progressively incorporated the neighbouring buldings, and, in much the same way as other powerful families of Siena, erected a kind of great, fortified town residence, called the «Castellare». The typically Sienese Gothic architectural elements are mostly 14th century, but there are several Renaissance additions as well. In 1781, Galgano Saracini enlarged the facade, conforming the whole to the more ancient part and the building underwent further heavy restructuring in 1923, when the painter, sculptor and architect Arturo Viligiardi turned his attention in particular to the concert hall, to which he gave a definitely 18th century flavour, even painting a great fresco on the ceiling vault in the style of Tiepolo which depicts the *Triumphant Return of the Sienese Army*

Above: **the Concert Hall and detail of St. Jerome, by Francesco Vanni;** *below*: **David and Bathsheba, by B. Mei** (Palazzo Chigi-Saracini).

after the Battle of Montaperti. The two modern bronzes that represent *Harmony* and *Melody* are by the Sienese sculptor Fulvio Corsini. The transformation was commissioned by Count Guido Saracini, last of his line, so that the famous **Accademia Musicale Chigiana** (Chigiana Musical Academy) should have a larger concert hall. The Academy was founded by Count Guido (who died in 1965) and has now become a State Recognized Moral Institution (Ente Morale) chaired by the President of the Monte dei Paschi di Siena bank, which partially funds it. The Musical Academy is considered one of the most prestigious in the world, not only because of the high quality of the concerts played within its precincts, but because of the hundreds of young musicians who flock to Siena every year from all over the world in order to

The Homage of the Magi, by Stefano di Giovanni (Palazzo Chigi-Saracini).

Via di Città with Palazzo Piccolomini.

The Fountain of the Contrada of the Eagle (Aquila).

Palazzo Chigi Piccolomini alla Postierla.

attend the master classes held in Palazzo Chigi Saracini by the most renowned musicians of our time. Thanks chiefly to the bounty of Galgano Saracini, Palazzo Chigi Saracini also contains a large and exceptionally interesting collection of Sienese paintings ranging from the 13th to the 18th century. The innumerable rooms of the mansion are furnished and decorated with hundreds and hundreds of *paintings*, *sculptures*, *furniture*, *objects d'art*, *porcelain*, archeological finds (*Etruscan urns, bucchero, vases* etc.), valuable *musical instruments*, etc.

Just beyond *Palazzo Chigi Saracini*, on the right, we meet the imposing **Palazzo Piccolomini**, called *Palazzo delle Papesse* (of the Women Popes), today headquarters of the Banca d'Italia, and one of the most perfect examples of Florentine Renaissance architecture, attributed to Rossellino. Via di Città ends in **Piazza Postierla** – also dubbed «i Quattro Cantoni (the Four Corners), where a column marks the Terziere di Città» (the third of the town named after the Roman town or 'civitas'). A vigorous stone *she-wolf of Siena* used to stand on the column but she has

Above: **Palazzo del Capitano**; *below*: the Residence of the Medici Governor.

Aerial view of Siena's historic centre.

since, for reasons of conservation, been placed inside Palazzo Pubblico. The modern little *bronze fountain* topped by an *eagle* (sculptor Bruno Buracchini), in the square, is one of the seventeen fountains at which the contrade's babies are given their «Contrada Baptism». The little fountain of the Quattro Cantoni is in fact where the children of the Noble Contrada of the Eagle are «baptised». One of the four corners of the square, the one on the left, towards Via del Capitano, is formed by the two façades of **Palazzo Chigi** and then **Piccolomini** (or *Palazzo Chigi-Piccolomini alla Postierla*), which is where the *Superintendent for the Artistic and Historical Assets of Siena and Grosseto* is quartered. The splendid mansion was commissioned by Scipione Chigi, towards the second half of the 16th cent.

probably to designs by the painter, sculptor and architect Bartolommeo Neroni, called Riccio. There are two more imposing buildings on *Via del Capitano*: on the right we have the **Residence of the Medici Governor**, which is used as the *Prefecture* and as headquarters of the *Provincial Administration*; on the left, the stony façade of **Palazzo del Capitano**, first built at the end of the 13th century as the headquarters of the War Captain and of the Captain of Justice. Like many other medieval Sienese mansions, this one also underwent heavy restoration. In 1854, the architect Giulio Rossi headed the restoration project, causing restructuring and additions. The ground floor is divided by nine Sienese ogival arches. The upper floor possesses nine twin-mullioned windows.

Piazza del Duomo.

PIAZZA DEL DUOMO

Via del Capitano leads into Piazza del Duomo, where the marble bulk of one of the most splendid and famous examples of Italian Romanesque-Gothic cathedral architecture towers above one. The present church (or rather the slightly smaller version formerly constructed on this site) replaced a pre-existing **Cathedral of Santa Maria**, built around the 9th century according to tradition, on the emplacement of a temple dedicated to Minerva. The façade of the new construction, also dedicated to the Madonna of the Assumption, and much larger than the primitive 9th century edition, was oriented towards the Hospital of Santa Maria della

Scala (as it is today). Tradition, supported by fairly credible documentation, affirms that the holy edifice was consecrated with due solemnity on the 18th November 1179. This building, too, however, except for the crypt, was totally restructured and enlarged as from 1215/20, bit by bit, so that regular services within the edifice should never be interrupted. Moreover, from 1316 onwards, the transept and apse were extended even further. The **Belltower** had already been grafted onto a pre-existing shortened tower-house belonging to the Bisdomini-Forteguerri family. The **dome** was finished in 1263, when it was covered with leaden sheeting and

Rosso Padellaio's «apple» or gilded copper sphere was placed on top. (one should bear in mind that the lantern was added much later – in 1667– in the «style» of the cathedral). Present art critics affirm that the innumerable instances of sculpture, reminiscent of Nicola Pisano's handiwork, such as those decorating the capitals in the front part of the cathedral was probably designed by the great Apulian/Pisan artist himself. The lower part of the **façade** was both designed and decorated with statuary by Nicola's son, the great Giovanni Pisano, who started working on the project in 1285. The extension of the transept and the elongation of the cathedral towards the choir started, it seems, towards 1316 and continued slowly until about 1339, met with so many technical and stylistic

View of the apse of the Cathedral, with the «Facciatone» (the great unfinished façade) to the left; *opposite*: **the façade of the Cathedral.**

obstacles that a commission headed by Lorenzo Maitani - Master-builder of the Cathedral of Orvieto in 1322 – decreed that it would be better to rebuild a new church «pulchra magnia et magnifica». The seed for the most ambitious and foolhardy enterprise ever undertaken by the Sienese had been sown, but many years were to elapse before it germinated. It was only on the 23rd August 1339, in fact, that the General Council of the Bell (Consiglio Generale della Campana) decreed the construction of a vast new temple, in which the existing cathedral was to be included as its transept. The first stone had already been laid some months before and work had started on the three gigantic aisles of the front section, which continued up to the Manetti or Santa Maria terrace

(piano) and were enclosed by the façade or «Facciatone». The ambitious plans of the Sienese were however disrupted first of all by the terrible «Black Death» plague of 1348, which decimated the population and finally by the collapse of certain essential parts of the construction due to irremediable technical deficiences, so much so, that in June 1357, the governors of the Republic were not only forced to decree the discontinuation of all work on the New Cathedral, but even had to order the destruction of all parts in danger of falling down. Important remains of the imposing temple are still visible today in the roofless area to the left of the existing cathedral (known as **Piazza Jacopo della Quercia**), with the columns of the three aisles, its unfinished

façade and a part of the left side, where a magnificent doorway (the most beautiful Sienese Gothic doorway and one of the finest in Italy) opens onto the steep staircase leading down to the Baptistery of San Giovanni. After interrupting the construction of the New Cathedral, the Sienese turned their attention once more to the old church, which reverted, this time definitely, to its rôle of Cathedral of Siena. Its façade was only completed towards the end of the 14th century. Work on it recommenced in 1377, under the Masterbuilder Giovanni di Cecco, who attempted to superimpose a late-Gothic top section with the central rose-window and three cusps upon the lower and older late-Romanesque section, spoiling the harmonious development of Giovanni Pisano's ar-

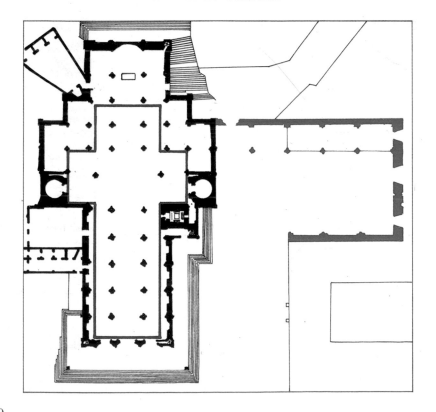

Above: the Pulpit, by Nicola and Giovanni Pisano; *below*: ground plan of the Cathedral and of its later enlargements; *opposite*: the awe-inspiring interior of the Cathedral.

chitectural elements, with the inert spread of the upper section which certainly owes much of its appearance to the Orvieto cathedral façade. Giovanni Pisano, together with helpers and followers, produced a whole series of marble statues of *Saints, Prophets, Sybils and Allegorical Beasts* which weave admirably and harmoniously in and out of the design of the lower façade. The figures one admires today are nearly all copies of the originals, which have been taken down and placed in the ground-floor room in the Museo dell'Opera del Duomo. The great spiralled columns, carved by Giovanni Pisano that used to uphold the main doorway, have been recently removed and will be replaced by copies. The architrave, sculpted by Tino di Camaino, a follower of Giovanni (c. 1297-1300), represents scenes from the *Life of the Infant Mary with St. Joachim and St. Anne*. The bronze doors with the *Glorification of the Virgin* are an unpretentious recent work by Enrico Manfrini (1958). Three mediocre mosaic panels by Augusto Castellani upon designs by Luigi Mussini and Alessandro Franchi (1877) were set into the cusps at the top of the façade during the 19th century. The mosaics, representing the *Coronation of the Virgin*, the *Birth* and the *Presentation of the Virgin at the Temple*, replaced three gilded bronze reliefs that had been made for the three cusps in 1635. The inlaid and etched marble panels in the parvis of the cathedral, led-up to by a stairway, are a kind of foretaste of the famous decorated floor inside the cathedral. At each end of the parvis, stands a column, bearing a *She-wolf feeding the Twins*, one attributed to the workshop of Giovanni Pisano, the other to Urbano da Cortona (the originals replaced by copies, are in the Museo dell'Opera too. The evocative, severely majestic **interior of the Cathedral** is enhanced by the forest of black and white marble striped pillars - the colours of Siena's «Balzana» or arms – which is a motif repeated throughout the building both inside and out. The black and white marble creates an impression of structural solidity, as well as providing a pictorial chiaro-scuro effect, that attenuates the vertical surge of the pillars surmounted by their rounded Romanesque-like arches. Before examining the

Above and opposite: **two views of the magnificent inlaid floor inside the Cathedral.**

daily wear and tear inflicted by thousands of visitors' and worshippers' feet. On certain very rare occasions, the floor is uncovered and is open to view. Among the scenes always left uncovered is the one showing the *Massacre of the Holy Innocents*, designed by Matteo di Giovanni (1482) and restored in 1790. It is probably the most admired scene on the whole floor (one of the reasons why it is left uncovered), because of its vivid colours and spectacular representation of violent movement. From the imposing, sumptuous interior, with its endless and somewhat boring line of *Popes' heads*, attributed (together with the equally lengthy theory of *Emperors' busts*) to the workshop of Giovanni di Stefano: they are terracotta busts moulded in the workshop and baked in the kilns of the Mazzaburroni family as from 1495 and coloured at the beginning of the 16th century. The asymmetrical *dome* is supported by six great piers. Two *wooden beams* lie between the two central piers (supported by them) which are supposed to have come from the «Carroccio» (War-Standard Chariot) used during the Battle of Montaperti (1260). Six gigantic gilded stucco statues of *St. Catherine, St. Bernardino* and the other four *Patron Saints of Siena* stand on top of the six piers. The right transept starts with the **Chapel of the Vow**, commissioned by Pope Alexander VII (Chigi) and probably designed by Gian Lorenzo Bernini, who was appointed supervisor of the construction of the Chapel (1659-'63). The ground-plan is circular; the Madonna and Child, venerated by the Sienese as the *Madonna of the Vow* (del Voto), above the altar, is the central portion of a much larger (no longer extant) painting attributed to the workshop of Guido da Siena (c. 1270). The Baroque of this shrine is decidedly Roman in flavour. The *shrine* surrounding the venerated 13th century image, the *gilded bronze angels* and all the *decorations* were designed by Ercole Ferrata from Rome and cast by Giovanni Artusi, called Piscina. The two large marble statues in the niches at the entrance are masterpieces by Bernini, himself, carved in Rome, between 1662 and 1663. They represent the *Magdalen* and *St. Jerome*. The Presbiterium is on a slightly higher level than the aisles and is dominated by the centrally

various works of art studded around the church, we should, at this point, pause to admire the unique artistic achievement we are standing on, which covers the whole floor of the cathedral, like some fabulous carpet: the 52 panels of **inlaid, etched and coloured marble**. The scenes in the central nave, starting from the entrance, depict *Hermes Trismegistus* (designed by Giovanni di Stefano), the *Sienese She wolf* with the *Symbols of the Towns allied to Siena* (14th century), the *Wheel with the Imperial Eagle* (14th cent.), the *Hill of Virtue* (designed by Pintoricchio); the *Wheel of Fortune and Power* (designed by Domenico di Niccolò?). The side-aisles contain the figures of the *Sybils*. Very little is left, unfortunately, of the original panels. The scenes beneath the dome, in the transept and in the apse are much better preserved. The greatest Sienese artists of the 13th and 14th centuries all contributed designs to this remarkable enterprise: great scenes teeming with hundreds of figures against the bristling towers of fortified towns and idyllic landscapes unfold beneath our feet all over the floor. Nearly all of them, unfortunately, are covered with planks of wood and sheets of cardboard to protect them from the

Above: **Chapel of the Vow and detail of the interior of the Cathedral;** *below*: **Candle-bearing Angel, by G. di Stefano and the High Altar.**

placed imposing marble and bronze **High Altar**, upon which stands Vecchietta's magnificent *bronze ciborium* (1472). Two bronze *candle-bearing angels* stand near the top of the steps leading up to the altar. They are the last admirable works cast by Sassetta's son: Giovanni di Stefano (1489). Francesco di Giorgio and Giacomo Cozzarelli made the other two *bronze angels* at the bottom of the steps, in 1490, endowing them with the same airy weightlessness that they gave the two little bronze *cherub-busts* (called «little spirits») springing from the great masks each side of the altar. Eight other *bronze angels* stand at the base of the pillars between the dome and the presbiterium, cast in 1551 by D. Beccafumi. The stained-glass **Rose-window** above the apse is of great interest, both because of its artistic merits as well as

Mystical Wedding of St. Catherine, by Pier Dandini and St. Bernardino preaching in Piazza del Campo by Sano di Pietro (Cathedral).

examples of Italian stained-glass. Carli dates it around 1288 and attributes the cartoon to Duccio, to whom most other critics attribute it, although others are more in favour of Cimabue and a helper. It used to be in the old apse and was transferred to the new one in 1365. It is divided into nine sections depicting: the *Burial*, the *Assumption*, the *Coronation of the Virgin*, the *Four Evangelists*, the *Four Patron Saints Ansanus, Savinius, Crescentius and Bartholomew*. It is almost a miracle that after so many centuries of wars and because it is one of the earliest known

destruction, such an extremely fragile masterpiece should have survived to shed its rainbow light on one of the most beautiful cathedrals in the world. The **Choir** (except for the 16th century choir-stalls in the apse-hemicircle) replaces a much more ancient 13th century choir, now lost. Francesco del Tonghio started working on it alone in 1362 and his son Giacomo joined him in his labours in 1378. Due to 16th century restructuring of the apse, a lot of the earlier ornamentation was unfortunately lost. The last important works on the choir, took place in 1813, when

the inlaid marquetry panels by Fra Giovanni da Verona were removed from the magnificent early-16th century choir-stalls which are still preserved in the Abbey-church of Monte Oliveto Maggiore near Siena, and grafted onto the 14th century choir-stalls in Siena cathedral. An interesting and little known piece of Baroque sculpture is to be found in the *Vestibule*, next to the sacristy: the *bronze bust of Alexander VII Chigi*, by Piscina. Beyond the **Sacristy**, decorated with frescoes attributed to Benedetto di Bindo (1212), we enter the **Chapter Hall**, hung with *portraits*

35

Above and below: **two views of the Choir Stalls in the Cathedral.**

of Sienese Popes and Bishops. The two most precious paintings in this room, however, are the delightful little panels by Sano di Pietro (c. 1444), showing *St. Bernardino preaching in Piazza San Francesco and in Piazza del Campo*. The latter is particularly fascinating, because the scene in front of Palazzo Pubblico is minutely described, as if it were the illuminated portion of a manuscript, with its groups of nobles and commoners, listening devoutly to the Saint. The larger group of the women is separated from the men by a long red curtain; the white shawls and veils draped over their heads half conceal long, embroidered red, black or green gowns of splendid effect. Sano has even painted the shutters on the windows, which enabled people to watch, without being observed, as well as the famous enclosure with its ladder, where a live wolf was kept as a symbol of the mythical origins of Siena we have already mentioned. Back in the left transept of the Cathedral, we find the staggeringly beautiful **Pulpit** by Nicola and Giovanni Pisano, the most superb masterpiece that adorns the Cathedral of Siena. A veritable milestone in the history of Italian art, it was, in truth, «the new art made visible». The great marble complex, covered with figures illustrating the history of the Redemption of Mankind, was started in Pisa by Nicola on the 29th September 1265 and continued in Siena the following year. It was completed by the 6th November 1268. Nicola Pisano was helped by his son Giovanni, Arnolfo di Cambio, Donato and Lapo. The three greatest sculptors of their time (Nicola, Giovanni and Arnolfo) worked side by side on this incomparable masterpiece, which although inspired by Nicola's own hexagonal pulpit in the Pisa Baptistery, is so much richer and more complex (about 307 human figures or heads plus about 70 animal figures or heads have been counted) as well as being less classical and more densely human in the intense expressive qualities of the faces and attitudes of the figures. A vibrant chiaro-scuro and a decided plasticity enhance the profound drama of the scenes (specially where Giovanni's chisel dug into the gleaming marble). The seven main panels on the balustrade, divided by the figures of the *Madonna*, *Christ*, *St. Paul*, the *Evan-*

Above: **St. Ansanus baptizing the Sienese, by Francesco Vanni** (detail) **and the Rose-window by Duccio di Buoninsegna;** *below*: **detail of the Crucifixion from the Pulpit by Nicola and Giovanni Pisano.**

gelists and *Trumpet-blowing Angels* are representations of Episodes in the Life of the Redeemer: the *Nativity*, the *Adoration of the Magi*, the *Presentation at the Temple*, the *Escape into Egypt*, *Massacre of the Holy Innocents*, *Crucifixion*, the *Elect*, the *Damned*.

In the left transept, opposite the Chapel of the Vow, we find the **Chapel of St. John the Baptist**, commissioned by the Rector of the Cathedral Works, Albereto Aringhieri, in 1492, as a worthy receptacle for the relic of the Baptist's Arm, preserved in a splendid 15th century *silver reliquary* and donated to Siena by Pope Pius II. The Chapel was probably designed by Giovanni di Stefano and has a circular ground-plan. The magnificent marble

doorway with statues and reliefs was carved by Marrina but the bases of the two *columns*, richly decorated with *classical motifs*, are by Antonio Federighi and Giovanni di Stefano. The elegant *bronze gate* is by Sallustio Barili. The great statue of *St. John the Baptist* by Donatello dominates the Chapel from its niche opposite the entrance. It resembles the wooden St. John in Santa Maria Gloriosa dei Frari in Venice and the wooden Magdalen of the Florentine Baptistery. The same dramatic feeling emerges from all their haggard visages, emaciated flesh and from the ragged locks of their hair and hair-shirts. An *octagonal marble holy-water stoup* with eight bas-relief panels by Antonio Federighi (1460) is placed in

Left: **Pulpit, by Nicola and Giovanni Pisano;** *below*: **detail of the Redeemer.**

St. John the Baptist, by Donatello.

Chapel of St. John the Baptist (Cathedral).

the middle of the chapel; the episodes depicted are: *Creation of Adam and Eve, Temptation of Eve, Appearance of the Almighty, the Expulsion from Eden, Herakles and the Lion, Cacus (or Herakles?) fighting a Centaur. Cherubs, dolphins, dragons* ect., decorate the base. We now come to another magnificent architectural, sculptural and frescoed complex made for the Cathedral, known as the **Piccolomini Library**. It was in fact commissioned in 1492 by the Archbishop of Siena, Cardinal Francesco Piccolomini Todeschini

(later Pope Pius III), who wished to create a worthy receptacle for the fabulous book collection put together by his uncle Pius II, who had died in 1469. The arch on the left, and the bronze *door* by Antoniolo di Giacomo lead into the Library, which was never in effect used for Pius II's books, but which was dazzlingly frescoed by Pintoricchio all over its ceiling and walls between 1502-03 (ceiling) and 1505-1507 (walls) after the death of pope Pius III. With the help of a large group of helpers, Pintoricchio recounted the

more salient events in the Life of Pius II. The picturesque and colourfully portrayed events seize both the simple and the cultured viewer with delight. Hundreds of figures, mostly in rainbow-hued ceremonial robes (the tints of which are so perfectly preserved, that they seem to have just been painted), throng the walls and are somewhat emotionless but nonetheless of highly spectacular effect. The ceiling is decorated in the Roman Renaissance fashion with «grotesques» arranged around the centrally placed device of Cardinal Pic-

Above: **Homage of the Magi, by Pietro Sorri and the Piccolomini Altar, by A. Bregno;** *opposite*:
the Piccolomini Library with the Pintoricchio frescoes (Cathedral).

colomini. The ten *Stories* on the walls, starting from the end, right of the window, can be thus described:
Enea Silvio Piccolomini, aged 27, leaving for Basle; E.S.'s oration in front of James I of Scotland; Frederick III crowns E.S.P. Poet Laureate; E.S.P. bows in submission before the true pope Eugene IV; E.S., as Bishop of Siena meets Frederick III, affianced to Eleonora of Portugal at the Camollia Gate of Siena.; E.S. appointed Cardinal by pope Callistus III; the Coronation of E.S. as Pope Pius II and his official entrance into the Lateran Basilica; Pius II assembles the Christian princes in Mantua, for the Crusade against the Turks; Pius II canonises St. Catherine of Siena, lying after death at his feet – on

the 29th June 1461 (it is said that the youth on the left, in the foreground is a portrait of Raphael and the likeness is in effect quite noticeable); *Arrival of Pius II, already very ill, at the harbour of Ancona to meet the Venetian fleet before its departure for the Crusade*. He was to die in Ancona, after waiting in vain for the fleet to arrive, on the 15th August 1464.
Vasari states that the cartoons for the frescoes were prepared by Raphael. Three drawings in the Uffizi seem to confirm this theory. The marble group of the **Three Graces** in the centre of the Library has been recently restored. It was brought from Rome by Cardinal Todeschini and donated to the Library. It is considered one of the best Roman

copies (among the eight known to be in existence) of a Greek painted or sculpted original. The most admired, after Pintoricchio's frescoes all around the room, are the great **missals** and **antiphonaries**, in the glass cases beneath the frescoes. The dazzlingly illuminated pages can rightly be considered some of the most important examples of the great Italian illuminators' art of the 15th century. Michelangelo Buonarroti left four statues in the niches of the great marble frontal, known as the **Piccolomini Altar**. Cardinal Piccolomini Todeschini, himself, commissioned it from the Lombard artist Andrea Bregno (c. 1480), who worked on it together with a series of helpers until his death (1501), filling it with exquisitely carved

statues and reliefs that remind one of Santa Maria del Popolo in Rome. It was probably the death of Bregno that induced Cardinal Todeschini to order 15 statues first from Pietro Torrigiani and then from Michelangelo Buonarroti, who, between 1503 and 1504, carved the statues of *St. Peter, St. Paul, St. Pius* and *St. Gregory* The statues are some of Michelangelo's less known works and we must admit that notwithstanding the plentiful and detailed documentation identifying them as his production, they show Michelangelo at his weakest and most uncertain, which may be due to the fact that he used helpers (specially in the case of St. Pius and St. Gregory). Both St. Peter and St. Paul are more truly Michelangelesque, in their vibrant torsion and in the energetically expressive decision of their stance, which evokes the overpoweringly dominant Moses of San Pietro in Vincoli in Rome.

Façade of the Hospital of Santa Maria della Scala and Candlebearing Angel, by A. Baldi (Church of the Hospital**).**

SANTA MARIA DELLA SCALA HOSPITAL

The long, low façade of the **Archbishop's Palace** runs along the left side of Piazza del Duomo (if one is looking at the Cathedral façade), and used (before 1660) to be the residence of the Operaio (or Comptroller/Overseer of the Cathedral Works) as well as of the Cathedral Canons, linked to the Duomo by means of a loggia. Opposite the Cathedral is the lengthy façade of the **Hospital of Santa Maria della Scala**. This august charitable institution was founded in the 9th century, although the first parchment document referring to it, officially legitimises the institution as late as 1090. At first, it was merely a hospice, but it was already a hospital in the 10th century, run by the Canons and later by lay brothers (Oblates) guided by a Comptroller or Rector. The name of Santa Maria della Scala certainly derives from the fact that it abuts on the stairs (scale) leading up to the parvis of Santa Maria, i.e.: the Cathedral. The building is immense, virtually a city within the city, where each century – for almost a thousand years – has brought additions and restructuring in its train, although the richly frescoed ancient 14th/15th century nucleus (the **Pilgrims' Hall** and the **Large Sacristy**), together with its irregular façade abutting on Piazza del Duomo have been preserved. The present **Church of the Hospital**, dedicated to the Virgin of the Assumption, is an enlarged, or rather totally reconstructed 15th century edition of a much smaller medieval church. The airy, simple interior fits beautifully into the aisleless Sienese Renaissance structure, reminiscent of the Franciscan Gothic tradition. The High Altar, a fascinating architectural and sculptural complex, bears an imposing bronze *Resurrected Christ* (1476) by Vecchietta, which replaced the ciborium by the same artist, which was transferred to the High Altar of the Cathedral in 1506. The statue is one of the finest of the Sienese Renaissance, possessing a Donatello-like dramatic quality, combined with exquisite anatomical technique and vigorous luminous effects. The two bronze *candlebearing angels* on the steps below were cast (1585) by Accursio Baldi da Monte San Savino, earning Giambologna's admiration and praise. The spacious apse hemicircle, once frescoed by Francesco di Giorgio Martini and enlarged and refrescoed by the Neapolitan painter Sebastiano Conca, who painted the *Pool of Bethesda* beyond a delightful colonnaded perspective fugue. A little door leads out of the choir into the sacristy/treasure vault, where a large number of reliques are kept in gold or silver *reliquaries* made by Byzantine and 15th-16th cent. Sienese goldsmiths.

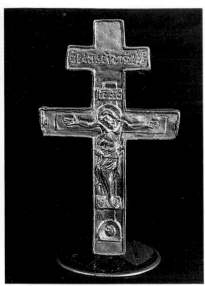

Above: **double-armed 12th cent. crucifix and reliquary chest** (Church of the Hospital); **the Enlargement of the Hospital, by Domenico di Bartolo** (Pilgrims' Hall); *below*: **Archbishop's Palace and Madonna and Child, by Paolo di Giovanni Fei** (Chapel of the Hospital).

Above: **David, by Carlo di Andrea Galletti; detail of an illuminated manuscript, by D. Beccafumi; detail of a fresco by L. di Pietro** (Church and Hospital of Santa Maria della Scala); *below*: **bird's eye-view of piazza Jacopo della Quercia.**

OPERA DEL DUOMO MUSEUM

The right aisle of the New Cathedral was transformed, as early as the 15th century into the headquarters of the Opera (Cathedral Works). Nearly all the rooms inside are now used for the Museum of the Opera del Duomo, which is chiefly famous for Giovanni Pisano's marble statues and for the great Duccio di Buoninsegna Altarpiece. Most of the ground floor is occupied by architectural fragments and by the great marble statues carved by Giovanni (1284/96) and his followers for the Duomo façade: powerful, dramatic figures of *Prophets, Sybils, Philosophers*, impetuosly launched forward or drawn inwards by their writhing muscles within the flowing flurry of their robes. An awesome concert of violently agitated figures, that nearly all express tragedy or terror, in gesture or expression: *Moses, Plato, Simeon, Elijah, Balaam, Miriam, Habbakkuk.* Even the *animals* seem to explode with tension in the complexity of their violently tragic masks that belong to a lost world of giants. The Duccio Room, upstairs, can almost be termed a Holy of Holies of ancient Sienese painting. After many adventures, the imposing **Duccio Maestà** has been placed here. It was commissioned from Duccio on the 9th October 1308 and the great panel was painted on both sides, with a predella and cusp decorations on both sides as well. Nearly all the painting was carried out by Duccio personally, as his contract stipulated. The front panel shows the *Madonna, Protectress of Siena, with her Son on her knees, seated on a throne and surrounded by a throng of Angels and Saints* – the first four kneeling figures are the Patron Saints of Siena: *Saints Ansanus, Savinius, Crescentius and Victor*. The predella contains seven little scenes from the *Life of the Virgin and the Infancy of Christ* spaced by the *figures of Prophets*. The cusps are decorated with further *Episodes from the Life of the Virgin*. The other side, that used to be turned towards the choir, contains innumerable *Scenes from the Life of Christ*. Even in its present denuded state, Duccio's Maestà is still one of the most remarkable turning points of European culture at the beginning of the 14th century, when profound transformations affected

Above: **the right aisle of the New Cathedral containing the Opera del Duomo Museum;** *below:* **the Duccio di Buoninsegna Maestà.**

every aspect of Western cultured mores. Where Giotto or Dante and even Giovanni Pisano opened-up vistas of unhoped-for human – albeit dramatic – earthly understanding, Duccio turned his attention towards a musical accord between heaven and earth, abandoning the conventional chains that had hitherto entrammelled the Byzantine heritage and directed his art towards more concrete forms, both in his transcendant poetic dreams of divine light, which he expresses in the gold leaf and lucid purity of his colours, as well as in the human reality of his solidly composed figures and their severely solemn expressions. A third masterpiece from the Duomo is preserved in the Duccio

Scenes of the Passion of Christ, painted by Duccio on the back of the Maestà Altarpiece.

Room: the *Birth of the Virgin*, by Pietro Lorenzetti, signed and dated 1342. Pietro almost anticipates the rediscovery of the rules of perspective of the following century and offers us a scene that is based on sapiently measured space (he has even broken with the tryptych tradition) and each pleasantly

leasured figure acts out its sacred rôle in composed solemnity. St. Anne is shown in the reclining position used for the statues of the deceased on Etruscan sarcophagi. In the two neighbouring rooms leading out of the Duccio room: various interesting reliques and artwork linked to the history of the Cathedral of

Siena. A famous group of five gilded wooden statues from the Church of San Martino, representing the *Madonna and Child, Saints Bartholomew, Anthony Abbot, John the Baptist and John the Evangelist*, attributed to Jacopo della Quercia and Giovanni da Imola has been placed in the vestibule of the right-

Christ before Pilate the second time	Flagellation	On the way to Calvary	Crucifixion	Burial	The Maries at the Sepulchre	Christ at Emmaus
Christ before Herod	The Crown of Thorns	Pilate washing his hands		Deposition	The descent into Limbo	Noli me tangere

Christ entering Jerusalem	The Washing of the Feet	Judas receiving the thirty silver pieces	Christ is arrested	Christ before Annas	Christ is beaten	Christ at the Praetorium
	Last Supper	Christ comforting the Apostles	Christ in the Garden of Getsemane	Peter's first denial	Christ before Caiaphas	Christ before Pilate

Above: **Birth of the Virgin, by P. Lorenzetti and Reliquary of St. Gawain;** *below*: **Madonna and Child enthroned with Saints, by Matteo di Giovanni and St. John the Baptist, by Francesco di Giorgio Martini** (Opera del Duomo Museum).

Drawing for the façade of the Baptistery (14th cent.); Madonna and Child and St. John the Baptist, by J. della Quercia (Opera del Duomo Museum).

hand room. Jacopo and his workshop are also supposed to have carved the much discussed painted wooden statue of *St. John the Baptist*, which comes from the Church of San Giovanni. The Treasure Room contains a large collection of gold and silver artefacts, most of which come from the Cathedral, even if the most precious and fascinating of all is the **Reliquary of the Head of St. Gawain**, that originally came from the great Cistercian Abbey of St. Gawain (San Galgano). This precious octagonal, cusped, shrine-shaped object chiselled in a style that is already Gothic, was made of gilded, embossed and filigree silver in the 13th century, almost certainly by French craftsmen. Pope Alexander VII Chigi also gave the Metropolitan Cathedral of Siena a *Golden Rose Bush* (cnd casc) which is like the one given by Pope Pius II Piccolomini to the Senate of the Sienese Republic in 1458, but with rather more

Illuminated manuscript showing Christ entering Jerusalem and the Golden Rose Bush donated by Pope Alexander VII (Opera del Duomo Museum).

Wooden Crucifix, by G. Pisano and St. Catherine of Alexandria, by A. Lorenzetti (Opera del Duomo Museum).

Left: **the great façade of the New Cathedral;** *right*: **the steps leading up from the Baptistery of San Giovanni Battista to the lovely doorway designed by Giovanni di Agostino.**

branches, leaves and roses. The last two rooms of the Museum have been placed almost at the top of the left aisle of the «New Cathedral» so that one has a close-up view of the great windows and magnificent capitals surmounting the black and white pillars incorporated in the building later on. The last room of the Museo dell'Opera contains a number of paintings, some of which can be considered absolute masterpieces. It is called the room of the *Madonna of the large eyes* (occhi grossi) or Madonna of the Victory of Montaperti. The importance to Siena of this venerable relique (the central part of an altarpiece) is certainly significant, if, as appears likely, this was the image placed on the high altar of the Cathedral, in front of which the Sienese vowed they would present the keys of the city to the Virgin (on the eve of the Battle of Montaperti - 4th September 1260) if they should be victorious against the Florentines, which in fact duly happened. The panel is assigned to an unknown artist (c. 1220/30).

Above: **the Articles of the Creed with the Resurrection of Christ, by Vecchietta and the façade of the Baptistery;** *below*: **Annunciation to Zacharias, by J. della Quercia** (detail from the Baptisimal Fonts).

SAN GIOVANNI BATTISTA

After the apse of the Cathedral was lengthened, abutting on the cliff over Valle Piatta, great arches were built beneath it, as from 1316, underneath which, a kind of new crypt came into being, called the Church of St. John the Baptist (San Giovanni Battista) – which was used as the Baptistery of Siena. Camaino di Crescentino was probably the designer of this new church. The six vaults of the Cathedral above St. John's were closed-up after the project of the New Cathedral was suspended, whilst the decoration of the façade of St. John's was continued for decades, under the direction of Domenico di Agostino, as from 1355. The top part of the façade was never finished, but the rest is in pure Sienese Gothic style, with three deeply splayed jambed doorways, above which runs a gallery of hanging arches and a frieze supporting three great twin ogival mullioned windows

Left: **Birth of the Baptist, by Giovanni di Turino**; *right and opposite*: **two views of the interior of the Baptistery.**

(1355). The three scenes etched into the paving of the parvis portray the *Birth of a Child, the Christening and the Blessing (or Confirmation?) of Six Young Children*. The interior of San Giovanni is rectangular, divided into three aisles by two broad pillars. All the vaults were completely frescoed in the 15th century; the most remarkable group of frescoes are the ones covering the central vault, by Vecchietta (1450) depicting the *Apostles* and the *Articles of the Creed*. The great masterpiece the world envies Siena, however, is the **Baptisimal Font** in the centre of the church. It has often been called the «oldest anthology of early Italian Renaissance sculpture». The magnificent complex was in fact enriched by a number of less famous artists, as well

as by the genius of three of the greatest sculptors of the time: Donatello, Lorenzo Ghiberti and Jacopo della Quercia. The base consists of two great hexagonal marble steps; the marble font itself is hexagonal too, the six sides, separated from each other by six gilded bronze figures of the *Virtues* contain six gilded bronze panels depicting, in chronological order, *Episodes from the Life of St. John the Baptist: Zacharias being told of the forthcoming birth of the Baptist* (Jacopo della Quercia); statuette of *Justice* (Giovanni di Turino); *Birth of the Baptist* (Turino di Sano and Giovanni di Turino); statuette of *Charity* (Giovanni di Turino); the *Baptism of Christ* (Lorenzo Ghiberti); *Faith* (Donatello); the *Baptist before Herod* (Lorenzo Ghiberti); *Hope* (Do-

natello); the *Head of the Baptist presented to Herod* (Donatello); *Fortitude* (Goro di Neroccio). The most impressive of all the scenes is the Donatello relief: a kind of vortex centred on the head of the Baptist seems to be whirling around the front scene. Each figure in the group on the right, divided from the focus of the scene by the perspective fugue of the floor, stands frozen in violent reaction to the horror presented to King. The background is a dazzling technical masterpiece of perspective planes etched-out in a few millimetres of bronze, where the life of the court continues imperturbably under the retreating arches, acted out by figures with timeless features that remind one of the profiles chiselled into ancient seals or medallions.

Above: **the headquarters of the National Picture Gallery in via San Pietro;** *below*: **detail from the Annunciation, by the Master of San Pietro** (National Picture Gallery).

NATIONAL PICTURE GALLERY

If one walks back along Via del Capitano, one encounters Piazza Postierla with Via di San Pietro leading out of it. The two mansions which used to belong to the Brigidi and Buonsignori families have now become the **National Picture Gallery** (Pinacoteca Nazionale di Siena), one of the greatest Italian museums, specially as regards the so-called «fondi oro» (golden backgrounds) of the Sienese 14th and 15th centuries. The Sienese painting tradition from Duccio di Buoninsegna to the Lorenzetti, from Simone Martini to Sassetta, Francesco di Giorgio or Giovanni di Paolo (including Neroccio, Matteo di Giovanni, Sodoma and Bec-

cafumi) is presented in chronological order, offering the viewer a fabulous series of masterpieces and minor works and a unique insight into the evolution of the painting art in Siena. The original nucleus of the «Galleria d'Arte» (Art Gallery) was instituted by Abate Giuseppe Ciaccheri (1723 1804), who assembled a certain number of paintings by early Sienese masters in the rooms of the old University. In 1816, Abate Luigi de Angelis, a professor at the same University, decided to re-arrange the paintings and founded the «Hall of Public Instruction» in Via della Sapienza. In 1847, the Superintendent of the Institute, Cavalier Alessandro Saracini, entrusted the researcher Carlo Pini with the chronological rearrangement of the collection. In 1866, the name of the collection was changed to «Galleria Provinciale» (Provincial Gallery) and more and more important pieces were added to it. On the 4th March 1915, the Sienese nobleman Niccolò Buonsignori left his mansion to the Provincial Administration, on condition that it be used as a museum or picture gallery. The events that led up to the formation of this important collection came to a head on the 15th May, 1930, when a decree was issued, officially authorizing the transferral of the National Picture Gallery of Siena to its present site in Via San Pietro. The Buonsignori palace, however, already appears to offer too restricted a space for the size and importance of the collection. The authorities are considering transferring the works to the Hospital of Santa Maria della Scala, in Piazza del Duomo, which is a museum in itself. The visit of the National Picture Gallery of Siena starts on the second floor. Further information on the works in the Gallery can be obtained from: P. Torriti, *La Pinacoteca Nazionale di Siena, I dipinti dal XII al XV secolo*, Sagep, Genova 1977; P. Torriti, *La Pinacoteca Nazionale di Siena, I dipinti dal XV al XVIII secolo*, Sagep, Genova 1978; P. Torriti, *La Pinacoteca Nazionale di Siena*, Genova 1982 (lst edition).

Right. The *Lent Altarpiece*, by Guido da Siena and *Madonna and Child*, by Duccio di Buoninsegna.

Miracle of Saints Cosmas and Damien, by Sano di Pietro. (Detail from a predella).

Above left: *Madonna and Child* attributed to youthful Simone Martini.

Above left: Detail of *Madonna and Child with Saints*, by Duccio di Buoninsegna. The quality in the central panel indicates the hand of Duccio himself, while the side-panels were probably by a helper.

Above: the *Madonna of Mercy*, from Vertine in Chianti, attributed to Simone Martini helped by Memmo di Filippuccio (the area with the people under the mantle of the Virgin). Masterpiece of fundamental importance for the study of Sienese art between Duccio and Simone Martini.

Opposite: The *Madonna of the Franciscans*, by Duccio di Buoninsegna. Notwithstanding its minute size, the spacious composition confers a stately monumental quality to the refined, exquisite draftsmanship of the painting. It can be considered one of the most masterly paintings produced between the 13th and 14th centuries by a young Duccio still under the influence of Cimabue.

Left: *Madonna and Child*, by Simone Martini. Discovered underneath a coarsely painted version from the end of the 16th century, she is considered one of Simone's most ethereal and fascinating feminine creations; could be dated around 1321 in view of obvious similarities with the polyptych in the Orvieto Museum and the one in the Pisa Museum.

Opposite: *The Blessed Agostino Novello*, by Simone Martini, with two details. From the church of St. Augustine, the great Altarpiece is now generally attributed to Simone before his departure for Avignon (1339). The delightful sequence of episodes and miracles from the life of Agostino Novello stresses the exquisite lyrical quality of Duccio's draftsmanship. The episodes illustrated are: *Healing of a child attacked by a wolf; Rescue of a child who has fallen from a balcony; Rescue of a knight who has fallen into a ravine; Healing of a baby who has fallen out of its cradle.*

Above, left: *Enthroned Madonna and Child with Saints and Prophets*, by Pietro Lorenzetti, known also as the Carmine Altarpiece, it has a predella illustrating the *Dream of Sobach; Carmelite hermits at Elijah's Fountain* (see detail below); *Pope Honorius III approves the Carmelite Rule*; the *Granting of a new habit to the Carmelite monks*. Ordered by the Sienese Carmelites, this fascinating altarpiece was painted by Pietro Lorenzetti in 1329, as the relative documentation and the dated signature confirm. Unfortunately, the work is incomplete, as two of the side panels and at least one of the cusps are today in American museums. The painting is nonetheless one of the most distinguished pictorial events in 14th century Italian painting, both because of its regal monumental quality, as well as because of the exquisitely defined details and landscapes in the predella.

Above: *Annunciation to the Virgin Mary*, by Francesco di Giorgio.

Opposite: *Adoration of the Magi*, by Bartolo di Fredi (second half of the 14th cent.). Considered this pleasing Sienese «illustrator»'s masterpiece.

61

Left: *Sea-town*, by Ambrogio Lorenzetti (also attributed to a 15th cent. artist, such as Sassetta). If by Ambrogio, together with the *Lakeside Castle*, would be the first two landscapes in European painting. On the other hand, perhaps, the scenes were part of a larger sequence, such as, for instance, a cupboard door. Their transparent draftsmanship and sapient light effects, providing the tremulously distinct glimmer with its cristalline reflexions so characteristic of Ambrogio.

Left below: *Madonna and Child with Saints Jerome and Bernardino*, by Neroccio di Bartolommeo. All preceding influences have been personalized by the artist, who offers us one of the most exalted instances of the whole of 15th century Sienese painting. The most immediate antecedent to this Madonna is Matteo di Giovanni's panel in the Opera del Duomo Museum, but Simone's lyrical profiles, painted some hundred and fifty years earlier already contain some of the lovable qualities of this Madonna by Neroccio.

Annunciation to the Virgin, by Ambrogio Lorenzetti. The last known work by this artist, who painted it for the Biccherna Magistrates of the Municipality of Siena. Interesting perspective study of the throne.

Madonna and Child, by Ambrogio Lorenzetti. One of the artist's most typical feminine figures and very reminiscent of the *Madonna of the Milk*, today in the Archbishop's Seminary in Siena.

Right: detail of the *Birth of the Virgin*, by Paolo di Giovanni Fei.

Top left: *St. Michael enthroned with Saints*, by Angelo Puccinelli from Lucca. Rare and splendid painting with gleaming lustrous gold backgrounds. Evident contacts with Simone Martini and the Lorenzetti brothers. Top right: *Madonna and Child* (detail), by Lorenzo Monaco. Left: *Last Supper* (detail of the Wool Guild's Altarpiece), by Stefano di Giovanni, called Sassetta.

Top opposite: *Madonna and Child enthroned* (called Piccola Maestà), by A. Lorenzetti and *Madonna of Humility*, by Giovanni di Paolo, below: *Madonna and Child with Angel*, by Francesco di Giorgio Martini and detail of the predella from the *Polyptych of St. Gawain*, by Giovanni di Paolo.

Above: *Madonna and Child with Saints* (detail), by Neroccio di Bartolommeo and *Episodes from the life of St. Blaise (The Saint fed by birds; the Saint and the poor widow)*, details of the predella, by Sano di Pietro.

Left and opposite: *Last Judgement* (detail) and *Presentation of Jesus at the Temple*, by Giovanni di Paolo. The predella of the Last Judgement reveals Giovanni's mature, lively, inventive style, and exceptionally transparent exquisite draftsmanship. The Presentation of Jesus at the Temple was commissioned in 1447 by the Rectors of the Corporation of the Pizzicaioli (Salted Meat and Cheese Merchants) for their chapel in the Church of Santa Maria della Scala.

Above: *Coronation of the Virgin*, by Francesco di Giorgio Martini: magnificent altarpiece, in which both the influence of contemporary Florentine artists, specially of Verrocchio, as well as the sinuous lines of his erstwhile companion-apprentice Neroccio di Bartolommeo are particularly evident. Top right: *Mystical Wedding of St. Catherine of Alexandria*, by Michelino da Besozzo, splendid example of the Late International Gothic Style. Right: *St. Jerome in the desert*, detail of the predella of the Osservanza Altarpiece.

Above: *Madonna and Child with Angels*, by Domenico di Bartolo. Signed and dated 1433, with beautiful Latin hexameters. This panel can be considered the highest expression of the Sienese Renaissance and even anticipates certain innovations introduced by Filippo Lippi and Domenico Veneziano. The early art of Donatello and Luca della Robbia's exalted cherubs in his famous choir balcony inspired Domenico as well as Masaccio's structured compositions and solid little babies, Domenico's Baby being the first of its kind in Sienese painting. Top left: detail from the *Flight into Egypt*, by Giovanni di Paolo, and bottom left: *Nativity*, by Lorenzo Lotto.

Above: *Holy Family with St. John the Baptist as a child*, by Pintoricchio; below: *Deucalion's Flood*, by Giulio Carpioni.

Above: *Announcing Angel*, School of Jacopo della Quercia; below: detail of the *Rebel Angels*, by Domenico Beccafumi.

Above: *Virgin receiving the Annunciation*, School of J. della Quercia; below: *Birth of the Virgin* (detail), by Domenico Beccafumi.

Above: *Adoration of the Child,* by Antonio Bazzi, called Sodoma; below: *the Tower of Babel,* by Flemish artist (beginning of 16th century).

Above: *Holy Conversation*, by Paris Bordone; left: *Flight of Aeneas from Troy*, fresco detached from the mansion of the Magnifico Petrucci, by Girolamo Genga.

Opposite, above: the *Stigmata of St. Catherine*, by Domenico Beccafumi and *Decollation of St. John the Baptist*, by the «Master of the Historia Friderici et Maximiliani»; below: detail of the *Rape of Europa*, by Johan Koenig and *Annunciation*, by Paris Bordone.

73

Above: **San Niccolò al Carmine and the Madonna of the Mantellini (Odighitria);** *below*:
detail of St. Michael and the rebel angels, by D. Beccafumi (San Niccolò al Carmine).

SAN NICCOLÒ AL CARMINE

Via San Pietro leads into Piazza di Postierla («I quattro Cantoni» or the «Four Corners»). On the corner, opposite Palazzo Borghesi, which used to contain frescoes by Beccafumi (now lost), is a *Chemist* containing interesting furnishings, designed by Agostino Fantastici, c. 1830. Turning immediately left, one enters *Via di Stalloreggi* («Stabulae Regis» or «Stables of the king»?), almost completely lined with *medieval mansions* built of brick or stone (where the towers of the Cacciaconti used to stand), which are often very interesting, as they have not undergone much restructuring and still preserve most of their original aspect. At the end of Via Stalloreggi, there is a gateway or arch, in the right pier of which a 16th century *shrine*, surrounded by a delicate stucco frame, encloses a frescoed *Madonna and Child, with Sts. John the Baptist*

Above: **Palazzo Incontri on Pian dei Mantellini and the Arch of the Two Doorways;** *below*: **the erstwhile church of San Marco; Via San Marco and the Oratory of the Contrada of the Snail (Chiocciola).**

and Catherine of Siena. Left of the arch, a plaque indicates that Duccio di Buoninsegna used to live in the house (probably after and not before painting the famous «Maestà», which «was painted in the Muciatti house outside the Stalloreggi gate», according to contemporary sources. The gateway belonged to the oldest circle of the town walls and consisted of two great arches, wherefore the gate is still known as the *Arch of the Two Doorways* (Arco delle due Porte). One of the arches has been walled-up for centuries. The most an-

cient *shrine* in town is set into the outer face of the town wall; it encloses a 14th century frescoed *Madonna and Child*. Leaving the archway, we turn left into the *Pian dei Mantellini* surrounded by churches and noble mansions. Of special note: the great complex of the *Carmelite Monastery* with the adjacent **Church of San Niccolò al Carmine**. The first documented proof of the Carmelite Order's presence in Siena and of the foundation of a church of theirs is dated 1262. The existing church was constructed through the 14th, 15th and

16th centuries and subjected to restoration and additions right up to the present century. The restored **Cloister** (Nr. 44), built at the end of the 16th century, contains frescoes by Giuseppe Nicola Nasini (1710), depicting scenes illustrating the *Carmelite Rule*. The *Belltower*, recently attributed to Peruzzi, seems in reality to belong to the 16th century, but is considered 17th century by other critics. The Carmelite Church, which managed to preserve most of its artistic treasures from the 19th century expropriations, and the radical restruc-

Above: **Martyrdom of St. Bartholomew, by A. Casolani** (San Niccolò al Carmine) **and the Chapel of the Rosary**; *below*: **Christ and the Virgin enthroned (c. 1270) in the Convent of the Clarissan nuns, near Pian dei Mantellini.**

turing at the beginning of the 20th century, is full of works of art. See especially: the great panel by Domenico Beccafumi, showing *St. Michael pursuing the rebel angels*, painted before 1535 and probably a second, expurgated version of the unfinished panel, now in the Pinacoteca (Picture Gallery) of Siena. Both of them are, at any rate, fundamentally important works of the Tuscan Mannerist school. The predella underneath is not original, but a mediocre contribution by Stefano Volpi. The Sacristy contains a beautiful statue in coloured terracotta of *St. Sigismund*, attributed rightly to Giacomo Cozzarelli in his late maturity (c. 1506). The Carmelite Church stands near the turning from Pian dei Mantellini into *Via*

della Diana, which takes its name from the spring that was hunted for in vain by the Sienese, as Dante Alighieri recalls. On the left, at the beginning, is the little Romanesque façade in black and white stone, of the de-consecrated church of San Marco, which is now used as a shop. The point at which *Via di San Marco* leads into Via della Diana is marked by the delightful little 18th century façade of the **Chapel of the Madonna of the Rosary**. The façade of the chapel is intact and is an interesting example of Sienese Baroque. Its design is attributed to Pietro Austo Montini (1722-23), as well as to Jacopo Franchini. The Renaissance well in front of the Chapel was commissioned by Cardinal Francesco Petrucci in 1522.

Aerial view of Sant'Agostino and San Giuseppe.

SANT'AGOSTINO

Via delle Cerchia connects Pian dei Mantellini with the **Prato di Sant'Agostino**, near the *Porta all'Arco* (Gateway of the Arch). It is a picturesque road that follows the line of the medieval walls. The imposing bulk of the **Church of Sant'Agostino**, the apse of which is still Romanesque, was started towards the middle of the 13th century (1258). Building went on, however, to such an extent that in 1309 it was still under way. We do not know exactly when work was concluded, but we do know that the church was enlarged and restructured between 1450 and 1458/90. Several important instances of this second period are visible on the outer walls of the Augustinian Monastery adjacent to the church, as well as inside the church itself, in the last chapel on the right in the transept, which was returned to its original state a few years ago. The overall impression one gains, inside this imposing church today – however – is that of a preponderantly neo-classical decor, with which Luigi Vanvitelli covered the ancient interior of the church in 1755, after the disastrous 1747 fire, totally renovating the build-

Above: **Madonna and Child, attr. to Giovanni di Turino and detail of fresco from the Piccolomini Chapel, by A. Lorenzetti** (Church of Sant'Agostino); *below*: **the Church of San Giuseppe near the Prato di Sant'Agostino and the Arch of San Giuseppe.**

ing and endowing it with a sober clarity and austerity of line that even manages not to clash with the monumental marble and «scagliola» – encrusted 16/17th century side-altars. One generally enters the church through the little door leading into the left aisle of the church from the «Prato» (field) di Sant'Agostino: which is an excellent vantage-point from which one can embrace all the numerous altar-panels painted by great Italian and (more specifically) Sienese 13th/17th century masters, e.g.: the *Baptism of Constantine*, by F. Vanni; *Trinity*, by P. Sorri; the **Bichi Chapel**, frescoed by F. di Giorgio Martini and Signorelli; the **Piccolomini Chapel** with A. Lorenzetti's *Enthroned Madonna* and the *Adoration of the Magi*, by Sodoma, etc. etc.

Aerial view of Fontebranda and the Basilica of San Domenico.

ST. CATHERINE'S BIRTHPLACE IN FONTEBRANDA

Back in Via di Città, we turn into the picturesque Via della Galluzza, to get to **Fontebranda** in the territory of the Noble Contrada of the Goose (Oca). Fontebranda takes its name from the most famous spring in Siena, but is still more renowned throughout the Catholic world, because it is where the Sienese Saint, Caterina Benicasa, was born. Her exalted religious fervour even shook Pope Gregory XI from his torpor. She was born in 1347, probably on the 25th March to the dyer Jacopo di Benincasa and to Monna Lapa Piagenti. The name of Catherine is especially linked to the history of the papacy, which, at that time, was quartered in Avignon. It was the mystical Sienese Saint who did

everything in her power to achieve the return of the popes to Rome (1371). Her famous «Epistles», full of ardent mystical passion, that she addressed – as Sister in Christ – to popes, princes and rulers all over Europe gave her literary as well as religious fame. She died in Rome on the 29th April 1380 and was canonized by the Sienese pope, Pius II Piccolomini in 1461. She was proclaimed Joint Patron Saint of Rome in 1866 by Pius XII and Joint Patron Saint of Italy in 1939. She was finally proclaimed Doctor of the Church in 1970 by Pope Paul VI. Catherine's birthplace was bought for the Commune of Siena on the 28th January 1466. The inhabitants of Fontebranda demanded

that it be placed permanently at the disposal of public veneration. Later on, the Confraternity of St. Catherine totally transformed the house into a veritable sanctuary, full of memorabilia and works of art dedicated to the memory of the Saint. The normal entrance to the Sanctuary of St. Catherine has always been on the Vicolo del Tiratoio. The beautiful Renaissance stone doorway is still visible, and one can read the words «SPONSAE KHRISTI CATERINAE DOMUS» carved into the lintel. Since the ancient parish church of Sant'Antonio was purposely demolished to construct in its place the so-called *Portico dei Comuni d'Italia* (of the Italian Municipalities) (1941), the entrance to St.

Above: **the Portico of the Italian Communes;** *below*: **the Keys of Castel Sant'Angelo being delivered to Pope Urban VI, by A. Casolani; Crucifix «of the Stygmata» (13th cent.); St. Catherine's Stygmata, by B. Fungai** (House of St. Catherine).

Catherine's House and its oratories has been through the Portico itself, and on the first Sunday of May, consecrated oil is offered by a different Italian municipality, every year. The only ancient element of this part of the complex is the fine travertine 15th/16th century *well*. Beyond the portico, there is a little *loggiaed hallway* with slim, elegant columns, generally attributed to Peruzzi. A second hallway, beyond the Peruzzi one, with arches at the end, links the Oratory of the Crucifix with the **Kitchen Oratory**, so-called, as it was partly built in what was probably the Benincasa kitchen. To start with, the room was the «Catharinate» Confraternity's prayer room; later, in 1546, it was enlarged by cannibalising various smaller rooms, whereupon the resulting enlarged chamber was richly frescoed. The **Church or Oratory of the Crucifix** shelters the 12th century Pisan school *Crucifix* that traditionally gave St. Catherine her «stigmata». Before leaving this mystical place, we need to mention the ancient **Fountain of Fontebranda**, which is downhill from the Oratory and next to the gateway named after it. It is the most famous, the most ancient fountain in Siena and its abundantly flowing waters have quenched the thirst of generations of Sienese, ground the flour of numberless mills driven by its flow, and provided a livelihood for innumerable wool-carders and dyers. As in all the most important medieval fountains, the first basin was used for drawing drinking water from; the second, fed by the overflow from the first, was the drinking trough for cattle and horses, whereas the third was used for laundry. Fontebranda, today, still has its three solid double, slightly pointed arches, enhanced by the red brick walls and by four stone lions. *Via dei Pittori* links the St. Catherine complex to *Via delle Terme* from which – at its end – one can turn into Via della Sapienza, on the left, which leads into **Vicolo della Pallacorda**, one of the most typical medieval alleyways in Siena. The beauty of its somewhat rustic architecture will both surprise and delight the visitor who takes the trouble to make the detour. The recently instituted **National Archaeological Museum** is in Via della Sapienza with the fascinating finds from Poggio Civitate near Murlo.

Above: **St. Catherine exorcises a possessed woman, by P. Sorri** (House of St. Catherine); *below*: **Fontebranda**.

Above: **Conversion of the prisoners condemned to death, by L. Bonastri and Wooden Statue of St. Catherine, by Neroccio di Bartolommeo** (House of St. Catherine); *below*: **Via della Sapienza; Vicolo della Pallacorda; St. Catherine gives the pilgrim Jesus a robe, by A. Franchi** (House of St. Catherine).

Aerial view of the Basilica of San Domenico.

BASILICA OF SAN DOMENICO

Via della Sapienza ends in the piazza of the Basilica of San Domenico, the construction of which, on the little hill called Camporegio, began around 1225, a few years after the founder of the Order, St. Dominic Guzman had been to Siena (1215?) (his visit is not documented, but is almost certain). The land for the church was donated by Fortebraccio Malavolti and the means were partly supplied by the Municipality of Siena and partly given in alms. The Dominican Church and Monastery must have been completed around 1262/65.

Towards the middle of the 14th century, the church was enlarged, as the fully Gothic style of the nave and of the transept reveals. The 14th century structure of the basilica is what we can admire today, even if it was disastrously damaged by a fire in 1443, which reduced it to a skeleton and by another in 1531, which started from a chapel and spread to the whole church. A raftered roof covers the vast aisleless

Left: **St. Catherine and worshipper, by Andrea Vanni;** *right*: **Birth of the Virgin, by A. Casolani;** *opposite*: **interior of San Domenico.**

nave, built in accordance with the monastic rule of the preaching order, so that the faithful and the preacher should not be separated by any structural obstacle. In 1667, the fresco of *St. Catherine and a follower*, unanimously attributed to Andrea Vanni (between 1375 and 1398) was moved to the **Chapel of the Vaults**, which has always been dedicated to the cult of the Sienese saint; Andrea Vanni was a faithful follower of the Saint, who wrote

him three letters, so we are moved to believe that the face of the Saint, at least, is the only portrait in existence, painted during her lifetime. Beyond the Chapel of the Vaults, on the right wall of the church, there is a succession of enchanting works of art, such as for instance, the *Birth of the Virgin* (1584), one of Alessandro Casolani's most beautiful paintings, justly considered his masterpiece. The **Chapel of St. Catherine of Siena** was commissioned

by Niccolò Bensi in 1460. The head of the Saint, brought here from Rome, in 1384, is on the splendid *marble altar*, sculpted in 1469 by Giovanni di Stefano, in the central niche, protected by a gilded grille and flanked by two sculpted candle-bearing angels; above the little window, there is a delicate image of the Saint surrounded by cherubim. The chapel walls are completely covered with frescoes each side of the altar, depicting the *Mystical Rapture of*

TVI · NICOLAI · SVSCIPE · CVRA

Left: **Mystical Rapture of St. Catherine, by Sodoma**; *right*: **the Shrine of St. Catherine, by Giovanni di Stefano**; *below*: **The Adoration of the Magi, by Matteo di Giovanni.**

St. Catherine and the *Exstasy or Eucharistic Vision of the Saint*. They are two world-famous masterpieces by this ardent painter who managed to effect a poetic blend of perfect draftsmanship with a sapient choice of colour, without ever falling into the trap of illustrative languor. Notwithstanding the restricted space at his disposal, the artist managed to impart a solemn grandeur to the monumentally silent figures. The *Adoration of the Shepherds*, by Francesco di Giorgio, is of exceptional interest, not only because of its high quality, but

Above: **detail from the Altarpiece of St. Hyacinthus, by Francesco Vanni**; *top right*: **Madonna and Child enthroned with Angels and Saints, by Benvenuto di Giovanni**; *bottom right*: **St. Barbara with Angels and Saints, by Matteo di Giovanni.**

also because it is one of the rare painted works of this great Sienese architect, sculptor and painter. Painted around 1475/80, the panel no longer reveals the influence of Neroccio, but possesses traits that bring it well within the sphere of Verrocchio, with its incisive lines, its classical landscape and its energetic realism, which we find again in Francesco di Giorgio's lovely panel of the *Nativity* (Pinacoteca of Siena); all these elements link the Sienese painter to the Florentine Renaissance at the end of the 15th century, between Verrocchio and Botticelli, when Leonardo's sublime spirit was spreading its wings. The fifth chapel, where the great altarpiece of Guido da Siena used to hang (now in Palazzo Pubblico), at present contains two ancient Sienese panel paintings; the first shows the *Enthroned Madonna and Child with Angels and Saints Gregory, James, Jerome and Sebastian*, and is one of Benvenuto di Giovanni's best works (1483) with its brilliantly clear gem-stone-like colours that throw the solid, massy figures into relief; the second shows *St. Barbara enthroned*

Madonna and Child, by Francesco di Vannuccio, surrounded by the Almighty with Saints Vincent, Ludovic, Catherine of Siena and Sebastian, by Sodoma and 15 little scenes from the Gospel by Sienese 16th century artist (San Domenico).

St. Anthony Abbot exorcises a possessed woman (detail), by R. Manetti (Basilica of San Domenico).

between the Magdalen and St. Catherine of Alexandria: probably Matteo di Giovanni's greatest work (1479); recently restored, it reveals a supremely luminous quality linked to delicate draftsmanship and a chromatic transparency that the Sienese artist had never before achieved (or was to achieve afterwards). Matteo also painted the enchanting *Adoration of the Magi* in the lunette above. The left wall of the central nave of the basilica is full of many other works of art, starting from the little panel on the first altar, by Francesco di Vannuccio (c. 1370/80) once attributed to Paolo di Giovanni Fei: it depicts a *Madonna and Child* and is grafted into the centre of a much larger panel, painted by Sodoma, representing the *Almighty, Saints Vincent, Ludovic, Catherine of Siena and Sebastian*. Below it, above the altar top, runs a predella divided into various orders, with *15 scenes from the New Testament* by an unknown Sienese 16th century painter, belonging to the Beccafumi or Riccio entourage.

Above: **the Medici Fortress of Santa Barbara;** *below*: **one of the rooms in the Enoteca Italica and view of the Gardens of the Lizza.**

FORTRESS OF SANTA BARBARA - PUBLIC GARDENS OF THE LIZZA

Leaving San Domenico, and going along Viale dei Mille one reaches the site of the erstwhile Spanish fortress of Don Diego de Mendoza, which was razed to the ground during a popular uprising in 1552, but then rebuilt a little further south by order of Cosimo I de' Medici after the taking of Siena in 1555. The Grand Duke personally entrusted one of his architects, Baldassarre Lanci from Urbino with the construction, in 1561. This powerful defensive and offensive instrument is rectangular-shaped, entirely built in brick and supported on an escarped base, surmounted by a thick bulging brick cordon. There are enormous, wedge-shaped bastions on each of the four corners with rounded spurs, surmounted by great *Medici escutcheons*. The extensive and fascinating underground chambers have been transformed into the cellars of the *Enoteca Italica*, which is famous for its Italian wine tastings. The **public gardens of the Lizza**, lying beneath the Medici fortress, were laid out in the 19th century.

Above: **Piazza Salimbeni with the monument to Sallustio Bandini;** *below*: **Antiochus on his sick-bed, by B. Mei** (Monte dei Paschi Coll.).

PIAZZA DEI SALIMBENI

Leaving Via Camollia, one goes down Via dei Montanini, which leads into Piazza Salimbeni. Today's Piazza Salimbeni was restructured quite recently – at the end of the last century – by the purist architect Giuseppe Partini. Most of the area it occupies was once the garden of Palazzo Spannocchi (on the right). The front section was a long corridor flanked, on the left, by the so-called Palazzo della Dogana (Customs), later called Palazzo Tantucci and at the end, giving onto the entrance into the Salimbeni Keep (Rocca), one of the most fearsomely fortified complexes in medieval Siena. After the 1264 and 1268 rebellions, the fortress was demol-

Above: the Hall of the Keep in Palazzo Salimbeni, the headquarters of the Monte dei Paschi bank; *below*: the Madonna of the cab-drivers and coachmen, by Giovanni di Paolo and Deposition from the Cross attr. to the Master of the Osservanza (Monte dei Paschi Coll.).

ished and rebuilt. Finally the Republic banned the Salimbeni family and confiscated all their possessions (1419). After it had been bought by the Monte dei Paschi (1866) for 60. 743 Lire, it was entrusted to the architect Partini, who restructured it adding on new wings and storeys in carefully imitated Gothic style. A *monument to Sallustio Bandini* (1880), sculpted by Tito Sarrocchi, was placed in the centre of the piazza. The present historical headquarters of the **Monte dei Paschi di Siena**, after the recent restoration by architect Pier Luigi Spadolini (1963/72), who managed to link the modern structures to the more ancient sections, includes the following 13th century organisms: the *Tower*, the *Salimbeni Warehouse* (Fondaco), the *Keep* (Rocca), Ranieri *Salimbeni's Little Palace* (Palazzetto). As well as the precious *Historical Archives*, which contain invaluable material for tracing the eco-

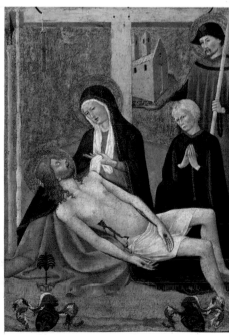

Madonna of Mercy, by Benvenuto di Giovanni (Monte dei Paschi Coll.).

nomic history of Siena, the Salimbeni Keep (Rocca) shelters a plentiful collection of works of art which the banking institution has amassed over the years. Thanks to the Monte dei Paschi's generous patronage, a large number of masterpieces that came into existence when Siena was a Republic, such as works by Pietro Lorenzetti, Sassetta, Giovanni di Paolo, Sano di Pietro, Beccafumi, etc. have been bought back and are to be seen in the Monte dei Paschi «Rocca» or Keep.

PIAZZA DE' TOLOMEI

From Piazza Salimbeni, one goes down Via Banchi di Sopra and one comes into Piazza dei Tolomei, with a column, surmounted by the *Sienese She-wolf*, by Domenico Arrighetti, called the «Cavedone». The piazza is named after the famous Sienese family – the most powerful one after the Salimbeni – against which it fought several times with a view to acquiring the overlordship of the town (it even claimed superior authority over the government). The great **Palazzo de' Tolomei**, which came into being after the Castellare (or Fortified Mansion) of the Consorteria dei Tolomei (which in 1290 included some 120 families) had been demolished. Notwithstanding the ruinous 1277 fire, the splendid building we see today is certainly one of the most noble in Siena, and probably dates back to 1270, with its elegant, twin-mullioned windows and the great hall on the ground floor which was restructured between 1430 and 1440), used today as headquarters of the Sienese branch of the **Cassa di Risparmio di Firenze**, where a number of sculptured fragments (*little capitals, lion-heads, the torso of a she-wolf*), that were found during the 1971 restoration works, have been placed on view. The square is dominated by the **Church of San Cristoforo**, one of the oldest in Siena (11th-12th century), famed for having been the headquarters of the

Piazza Tolomei with Palazzo Tolomei beyond the column with the She-wolf.

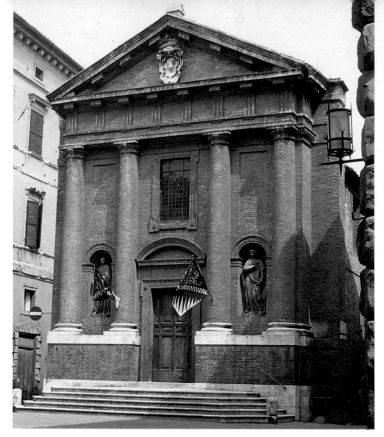

Left: **the façade of San Cristoforo;** *right*: **side-entrance to the church from Via Cecco Angiolieri;** *below*: **the little 13th century cloister.**

The Loggia of the Merchants
started in 1417 and designed
by Sano di Matteo.

Left: **Palazzo Spannocchi in Via Banchi di Sopra;** *above*: **interior
of the Loggia of the Merchants.**

Greater Council of the Republic (Consiglio della Campana) in the 12th and 13th centuries. Unfortunately, after the terrible 1798 earthquake, the church was shortened and was given its neoclassical façade, by Tommaso and Francesco Paccagnini, with the two 1802 *statues* by Giuseppe Silini and the *Tolomei escutcheon*. Next to the church is a charming little *cloister*, probably built around the beginning of the 13th century, with brick columns and stone capitals, unfortunately heavily restored in 1921.

SAN FRANCESCO

Behind the church of San Cristoforo, along Via del Giglio, one reaches Piazza San Francesco, where the Basilica of San Francesco stands. Anonimous Sienese chroniclers mention 1228 as the year in which the first church dedicated to St. Francis was built on the hill of the Castellaccia di Ovile (Castle of the Sheep-fold). The decoration of the rough stone façade with black and white marble stripes was started just before the end of the 13th century and discontinued after only half the façade had been covered and was never resumed. The church, on the other hand,

Above: **San Francesco today and with the earlier doorway in a photograph taken during the last century;** *below*: **interior.**

Above: **Crucifixion, by Pietro Lorenzetti;** *below*: **the great cloister in San Francesco.**

was enlarged, because it was too small, in 1326. Only the façade and the right flank of the ancient Romanesque church were preserved; the left flank was demolished once the new left wall had reached the roof. The presbitery was entirely rebuilt on powerful arches, surmounting a magnificent underground crypt nestling into the steep slope of the hill. In 1475, the new enlarged church was finished. Lastly, the walls were raised, in 1482, to match the increased width of the renovated church. Francesco di Giorgio was almost certainly the architect entrusted with the latter project. The lovely main outside portal, in purest Sienese Renaissance style, is worthy of his hand. The structural parts

of the church finished by Francesco di Giorgio are still visible today, but nearly all the treasures it used to contain were devoured by the terrible fire of the 25th August 1655, which even carbonised the marble and the altars. The few surviving paintings are now in the National Picture Gallery of Siena. In the (eighth) Bandini Piccolomini Chapel (dedicated to St. Bernardino), two great frescoes by Ambrogio Lorenzetti, depict the *Martyrdom of the Franciscan Friars* and *St. Ludovic, King of France, taking his leave from Pope Boniface VIII after abdicating his claim to the throne in favour of his brother Robert of Anjou.* Nothwithstanding their bad state of conservation, the frescoes are full of Ambrogio's inventive and delightfully realistic touch. The compositions reflect the spatial awareness we have observed in Ambrogio's Allegory of Good Government, in the Hall of Peace in the Palazzo Pubblico.

Above: **St. Ludovic takes his leave from Pope Boniface VIII, by Ambrogio Lorenzetti;** *below*: **frescoed polyptych, by Lippo Vanni and the apse of the Basilica of San Francesco.**

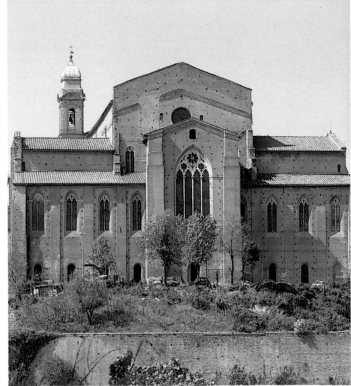

The square in front of Santa Maria di Provenzano.

SANTA MARIA DI PROVENZANO

Returning from Piazza San Francesco along Via delle Vergini, one reaches the Basilica of Santa Maria di Provenzano, in honour of whose much venerated image, the Palio race of the 2nd July is run. The Standard (Palio) is left in the church until the beginning of the race. On the 2nd July, it is taken to the Piazza del Campo and given to the winning Contrada, whereupon, amidst a turmoil of rejoicing members of the victorious Contrada and of the allied or friendly Contrade, the «cencio» (rag) is run back to the Basilica, to offer solemn thanks to the Virgin of Provenzano for the victory. The church was started in 1595, and, architecturally speaking, was completed in 1604. It was consecrated on the 16th October 1611. The design of the church is based on the Roman church of Gesù, designed by Vignola, that best conforms to the spirit of the Counter-Reformation: a single, shortened nave, for easier preaching and a series of side-altars, which are simply built against the side-walls of the church and not surrounded by separate chapels as they are in the 16th century Roman church by Jacopo Barozzi, known as Vignola.

Above: **the Logge del Papa (Pope's Loggias), by A. Federichi and the church of San Martino near Palazzo Piccolomini;** *below*: **detail from the Keys of Siena being offered to the Virgin, (1483) (**Museum of the tables of the Biccherna**).**

PALAZZO PICCOLOMINI

Proceeding towards Via Banchi di Sotto, one crosses one of the most fascinating medieval districts of Siena, which used to be where the great Castellari (Fortified Mansions) used to stand. Next to the erstwhile Castellare of the Uguccioni family is the seat of the **University of Siena**, and opposite the latter, the noble bulk of Palazzo Piccolomini, which hosts the *State Archives*. Started towards the middle of the 15th century, by Bernardo Gambarelli, known as Rossellino, it introduced the purest Florentine Renaissance civilian architecture to Siena. Rossellino was the architect Pius II Piccolomini commissioned to build his model Renaissance jewel-town

of Pienza. The State Archives of Siena contain the famous and unique collection known as the **Museum of the tables of the Biccherna** (tavolette della Biccherna). It includes 103 painted panels, which were the covers of the registers, as well as 2 painted canvases, which come from the Biccherna and Municipal Tax (Gabella del Comune), from the Hospital of Santa Maria della Scala and from other Sienese administrative archives. The Biccherna (the most important financial magistrature of the Sienese Municipality) adopted the practice – towards the middle of the 13th century – of having the covers of the most important registers in its offices painted. The pratice was also adopted by other financial magistratures and continued up to the 18th century. The collection constitutes a marvellously complete pictorial history of four centuries of Sienese life.

Right: **façade of the Palazzo Piccolomini;** *left*: **«Siena at the time of the Earthquakes» by Francesco di Giorgio Martini;** *below*: **interior of a Sienese bank (15th cent.);** *overleaf*: **the Virgin recommending Siena to Jesus** (Museum of the Biccherna).

HEC EST CIVI
TA MEA

QVESTI · SONNO · ENOMI · DIQVELI · SPETTABILI · CITTADINI · STATI
LLO · OFFITIO · DELI · EXEGVITORI · DICABELLA · GENAIO · 1479 · DAFINIRE
COME · SEGVE · PSEI · MESI · EPRIMA · MACTIO · DANTOGNIO · DINERI · CHA

Above: **the entrance to the Synagogue;** *below*: **an alley-way in the old ghetto;** *right*: **the interior of the Synagogue.**

SYNAGOGUE

The Jewish Temple of Siena, in the University district, was built in 1756, upon designs by the architect Giuseppe del Rosso in neo-Classical style. The wooden decorations were made by two master carpenters: Niccolò Ianda and Pietro Rossi. The columns flanking the Ark are supposed to have been made out of pieces of marble that came from Jerusalem and are particularly worthy of note. One of the finest surviving pieces of the original rich furnishing is the *Circumcision throne* which was made in 1860. The Temple follows the Sephardic rite. Six curiously fashioned marble cavities have been recently discovered in the entrance hall. They are dated 1600 and were used for collecting offerings and contributions for the Jewish community of the time.

Above: **church of the Prison (Carceri) of Sant'Ansano**; *below*: **San Giacomo in Salicotto.**

Above: **San Sebastiano in Vallepiatta**; *below*: **the Bishop's Palace.**

Above: **Via Cecco Angiolieri;** below: **Santa Petronilla.**

Above: **the Botanical Gardens of the University;** below: **the Fonte Nuova d'Ovile (New Fountain of the Sheepfold).**

Above: **San Pietro alla Magione;** *below*: **Porta San Maurizio, known also as Samoreci.**

Above: **aerial view of San Martino;** *below*: **Santa Maria delle Nevi (of the Snows).**

Above: **San Clemente in Santa Maria dei Servi**; *below*: **the Madonna of the Crow (Corvo), by Sodoma.**

Above: **the church of the Holy Spirit (Santo Spirito), with the Pispini Fountain**; *below*: **the Oratory of the "Tredicini".**

Via Campansi intersecting with via Camollia.

Above: the Church of San Pietro; *below*: Santa Maria degli Angeli in Valli.

Above: the Gateway of the Tufa-stones (dei Tufi); *below*: Palazzo della Consuma.

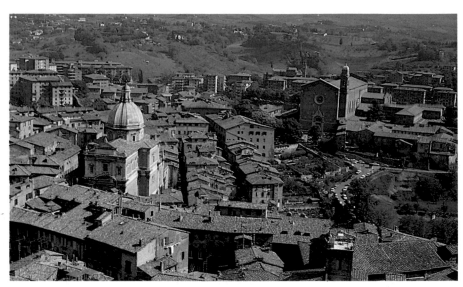

Above: the church of San Raimondo; *below*: Santa Maria in Portico near Fontegiusta.

Above: bird's-eye view of Siena with Santa Maria di Provenzano and San Francesco; *below*: the Salimbeni Keep.

Above: **the inner side of Porta Camollia;** *below*: **detail of the outer side of Porta Camollia.**

PORTA CAMOLLIA

Porta di Camollia, the strongest and most dreaded gateway of Siena opened onto and concluded the Via Cassia, that came from Florence. The gateway we see today was rebuilt in 1604, to designs by Alessandro Casolani. Its stone decoration was carved, according to the historical documents available, by Domenico Cafaggi, sculptor. The external arch of Porta Camollia bears the famous inscription which was carved onto it to honour Ferdinand I de' Medici's arrival in Siena: *COR MAGIS TIBI SENA PANDIT* (Siena opens her arms wide to welcome you). Outside Porta Camollia, one meets Villa Montarioso, which contains the **Museo Diocesano di Arte Sacra** (The Diocesan Sacred Art Museum), of great historical and artistic value.

Above: the outer side of Porta Romana; *below*: the court between the inner and outer gateways of Porta Romana.

PORTA ROMANA

Porta Romana (the Roman Gate) which belongs to the 14th century walls, is the largest of all the Sienese gates. It is provided with an imposing anteport and still boasts two stone *she-wolves* in the style of Giovanni di Stefano commissioned in 1467 and fixed onto adjutting stone shelves. The remains of a great fresco under the archway were removed some years ago and taken to the Basilica of San Francesco. In 1734, Cavalier Pecci inserted a *fragment of a Roman inscription* into the right side of the main archway, which recalls the cult of Augustus: «SILVANO SAC(RUM) / C.VICTREICIUS / MEMOR VI VIR (A)UGUSTALIS POSUIT» and confirms the expansion of Roman colonies to include the territory of Siena.

Above and below: **the roofs of Siena in summer and winter.**

Above and below: **two typical aspects of the Sienese countryside.**

TERZO
DI CAMOLLIA

TERZO
DI CITTA'

Left: *the Palazzo
Pubblico with the
Contrada banners
displayed during the
Palio; above: the
town of Siena
divided up
according to the
territories of the
Contrade.*

THE CONTRADE AND THE PALIO

The Contrade (Districts) of Siena were instituted between the end of the 12th and the beginning of the 13th century, with administrative (tax collection, road maintenance) and public safety (police) responsabilities, etc. These institutions, quartered in or around the parish churches, public meeting places or places of worship, were governed by a kind of mayor, who was answerable directly to the Podestà (Chief of Justice) and was assisted by councillors elected by the people of the Contrada. The structure of the Contrade was completed after the formation of Military Companies (the army of the Republic) which enrolled every able man from 18 to 70 years of age. The Military Companies were in turn grouped into the so-called «Terzi» (Thirds), corresponding to the three territories Siena had been divided into: the Terzo di Città (a white cross on red ground), the Terzo di San Martino (St. Martin and the beggar on a wine-red ground), and the Terzo di Camollia (a black K on white ground).

Each Terzo was commanded by a Master Standard-bearer (Gonfaloniere Maestro). The Captain of the People bore a standard with a Crowned Lion Rampant on red ground: he was the supreme Commander of the Militia. In the 14th century, the «fameglie» (clans) of Siena were distributed among the 42 Contrade, which were reduced to 23 between the 15th and 16th centuries. In time, the political and administrative reasons that had brought about the creation of the Contrade, became obsolete and the latter turned their attention more and more to the organisation of public games that had long been current in the town. The 23 Contrade took the names of *Aquila* (Eagle), *Bruco* (Caterpillar), *Chiocciola* (Snail), *Civetta* (Owl), *Drago* (Dragon), *Gallo* (Cockerel), *Giraffa* (Giraffe), *Istrice* (Porcupine), *Leone* (Lion), *Liocorno or Leocorno* (Unicorn), *Liofante* or *Torre* (Elephant or Tower), *Lupa* (She-wolf), *Montone* (Ram), *Nicchio* (Shell), *Oca*, (Goose), *Onda* (Wave), *Orso* (Bear),

115

The Cortège of the Contrade, by V. Rustici (Monte dei Paschi Coll.) ··

AQUILA (EAGLE)

CHIOCCIOLA (SNAIL)

BRUCO (CATERPILLAR)

CIVETTA (OWL)

The Bull-fight, by V. Rustici (Monte dei Paschi Coll.**).**

Pantera (Panther), *Quercia* (Oak), *Selvalta* or *Selva* (High Forest or Forest), *Spadaforte* (Strong Sword), *Tartuca* (Tortoise), *Vipera* (Viper). No documents exist explaining why the names (that were probably prompted by popular imagination or fancy or by some special event) were actually chosen. 1675 seems to be when six of these Contrade were suppressed, to wit: Gallo, Leone, Orso, Quercia, Spadaforte and Vipera.

The Contrade today

Each contradaiolo (contrada member) pays an annual contribution, called «protettorato» (protectorate). The organisation of the Contrade, as we have already mentioned, is mediated by various organisms created to cope with the various activities the Contrada decides to embark on. One of the most important sectors is the Young Members' activities, as the sons and daughters of the Contrada represent its «future». The young are schooled in the history of their own and of the other Contrade. The Women's Group in nearly every Contrada takes on the above task. The Women's Group is also entrusted with the preparation of the Children's Festal Banquets (one of the most important being annual feast celebrating the Birth of the Virgin on the 8th September, when the children of each Contrada deck-out their Contrada's shrine dedicated to the Virgin; in the evening, all the children sit down to a banquet laid out along the street). The most important festival is the feast-day of the Patron Saint of the Contrada (which is

DRAGO (DRAGON)

GIRAFFA (GIRAFFE)

ISTRICE (PORCUPINE)

LEOCORNO (UNICORN)

LUPA (SHE-WOLF)

NICCHIO (SHELL)

celebrated by nearly all the Contrade on the nearest Sunday to the Saint's day proper): the streets of the Contrada – are lit by the «braccialetti» (bracelets) – kind of wall-torches in carved wood, painted in the colours of the contrada – with bunches of light bulbs or little tallow lamps with great floating wicks that burn through most of the night. On the eve of the Feast-day, the Priore (Prior) of the Contrada, accompanied by the Seggio (governing body) and by the Popolo (People of the Contrada), receives the representatives of the allied contrade at the frontier of the Contrada. Preceded by a drum and by the standard-bearers, the procession goes to the Contrada's Oratory to sing Vespers. Afterwards, everyone pours out into the streets, where games are played, such as the «Children's Palio», the Sack Race and Climbing the May Pole and many others, invented by the Contrade. Above all, everybody sings a tune, which is common to all seventeen contrade, when «speaking of Siena», which is fitted to extemporary verses, praising one's own Contrada or denigrating its enemies. Then one drinks wine. Festivities go on until late at night. In the morning, mass is sung in the Oratory and the costumed Comparsa, consisting of dozens of drummers, standard-bearers, etc., leads the procession round the town, to pay tribute to the «protectors» (This tour is repeated on the following Sunday, only this time the procession walks around the outside of the medieval town walls, following the so-called 'giro di campagna' (country walk). Towards the late afternoon, the whole procession (Comparsa, Priore, Seggio and Popolo) triumphantly return to their own Contrada.

The Società di Contrada

The first Società di Contrada came into being in the 19th century and are in charge of the Contrada's yearly activities. They are generally based in rooms adjacent to the Contrada headquarters and generally include a communal room, where meetings, dances and various other events are staged; recreation rooms, a bar and a well-equipped kitchen. The activities they organise are many: cultural, sporty, social (e.g.: blood-donor groups). The bar and the recreation rooms are looked-after by the members of the contrada, who take it in turns (without any regard as to class or social standing and entirely voluntarily) to serve at the bar and the tables. The kitchen is mostly entrusted to the Women's Group, who use it for the banquets, specially the banquet on the eve of the Palio, if the Contrada is running, which is called the Cena della Prova Generale (Banquet of the General Rehearsal) when up to over a thousand people have to be fed.

The Carriera (Race) in the Piazza del Campo today – The «Drawing» of the Contrade

Drawing the Contrade by lots is the first act of the Palio, and is performed about a month before the race (the last Sunday of May for the July palio and the Sunday after the July palio for the August one). 10 Contrade take part in the race. The rules which govern the drawing by lots are in fact less complex than one might think. The seven Contrade which haven't run in the preceding July Palio are entitled to run in the July Palio of the following year. The remaining three places are assigned according to the luck of the draw, to three of the Contrade who did take part, bringing the number of the participants up to the statutory ten. The same method is adopted for the August Palio, wherefore the two Carriere (races) of July and August are totally unrelated to each other as regards the Contrade participating in them. A Contrada, for instance, might run twice in the same year, but would automatically be excluded from the two «carriere» in the following year, unless it were to be again drawn by lot. On the morning of the «Sorteggio» (drawing), the standards of the seven Contrade running in the next Palio by right are hung outside the first floor windows of the Palazzo Pubblico.

OCA (GOOSE)

SELVA (FOREST)

ONDA (WAVE)

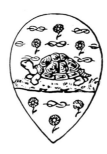

TARTUCA (TORTOISE)

PANTERA (PANTHER)

TORRE (TOWER)

The Piazza del Campo is prepared

For a Sienese, «Terra in Piazza» (earth on the Piazza del Campo) means Palio: joy, hope and rivalry. Shouts, invocations, throbbing songs surge from street to street, from square to square, up to the final explosion (this time, only in the winning contrada) after the race. These are the moments of greatest inner delight to a Sienese, and can only be compared to the moment in which the Palio is handed down to the winning Contrada in the «Piazza» and to the other moment of totally pagan exultation that assails the People of the victorious Contrada when they tumble into Santa Maria di Provenzano or into the Cathedral to offer thanksgiving for their victory. Several days before the race, the road around the «Piazza» is covered with a thick layer of tufaceous earth, which will enable the hoofs of the horses to «bite» the ground better. The stands for the spectators, the «Judges» stand, where the Captains and Lieutenants of the Contrade also have their seats, as well as the

VALDIMONTONE (RAM)

Above: the Festival of the Shrines in the "Eagle" Contrada. *Below*: the Piazza del Campo during the Palio.

The «Tratta» (Drawing of the Horses)

Four days before the Palio (on the 29th June for the July Palio and on the 13th August for the Assumption one), the «cavallai» (horse-owners), equipped with veterinary certificates, lead their horses into the Podestà courtyard of the Palazzo Pubblico, early in the morning. The municipal officials identify the horses with a number in progressive order called the «coscia» (flank) number, according to the order in which they are presented. A vet, appointed by the Town Council, checks the medical certificates and the state of the horses' health. After which, in lots of five or six at a time, the horses are taken out to show their paces by the owner's stable's jockeys or by the jockeys who ran in the Palio of the preceding year, who are at the disposal of the Town Council for the selection of the horses for the next Palio. The horses have to circle the track three times (about 1000 metres in all). After the trials, the vet checks each horse once again and the Captains of the Contrade running in the Palio choose the ten horses who will run in the Palio. In the meantime, a large number of «contradaioli» (contrada members) have gathered in front of Palazzo Pubblico to view the public assignment of the horses. The Mayor and the 10 Contrade Captains sit on a platform, set up in front of the Palazzo Pubblico, upon which stand two urns. The 10 selected horses are led into special horse-boxes installed left of the platform. The Mayor puts 10 numbers from 1 to 10 in one urn and the names of the 10 Contrade in the other. Two signboards hung above the platform against the Palazzo Pubblico wall, will show which horse has been allotted to which Contrada. Thereafter, even if the horse were to be prevented from running by some physical impediment or even by death, the Contrada would not be allowed to replace its allotted steed. The «barbareschi» (grooms who will lovingly care for their Contrada's horse up to the moment in which they hand it over to the jockey to run in the Palio), wearing the colours of their respective Contrada, each take charge of the assigned horse, and lead it to the Contrada's stable.

The Rehearsals, the Parties and the Palio

As from the afternoon of the day of the «Tratta» (selection) of the horses, the barberi (steeds) are rehearsed morning and afternoon, six times before the race, by the jockeys chosen by the Contrade, who try to get hold of the riders most likely to succeed (either because of their experience, familiarity with the horse or because of their weight). The Captains and their Lieutenants spend these days getting the «partiti» (parties/allies) together, bribing or planning how to damage the enemy contrade and above all how to win the race. The negotiations continue in absolute secrecy right up to the last moment before the Palio. At last the day of days dawns. Early in the morning, the Archbishop of Siena celebrates to so-called «fantino» (jockey's) Mass in the Cappella di Piazza (the Piazza chapel) and shortly afterwards, the last trial is run (called the «provaccia»), after which the jockeys that are taking part in the Palio are registered officially by the Town Council. In the early afternoon, each Contrada church is crammed full of contrada members, while the Correttore (Corrector) blesses both horse and jockey and in the throbbing silence cries the ritual propitiatory formula: «Go, and return victorious!». The «Comparse» of the Contrada start off, wearing their splendid costumes and waving their banners, for the Cathedral Square, where the Historical Cortège forms up in front of the Prefecture. It also includes the representatives of the Sienese Municipal Council, of the «Arts», of the «Studio Senese» (University), of the Municipal Councils of Massa Marittima and Montalcino, who took part in important events of Sienese history. Last of all comes the «Carroccio» (Standard bearing cart) – drawn by oxen and followed by a mounted escort of knights from the noble Sienese families – which

stand of the Priori are all set up against the buildings all around the square. The Judges' near the Costarella dei Barbieri (the horses' starting and arrival post), the Priori's near the Chiasso Largo. The shell-shaped centre of the square, capable of holding some 40.000 spectators, is surrounded with metal barriers. At the Costarella dei Barbieri, a contraption is set up, called the «verrocchio», which is the piece of equipment used by the «mossiere» (starter), who is the only person allowed to start the horses off: the «verrocchio» causes a thick rope (canapo) streched across the track, to drop suddenly, once it has been drawn tight by a winch situated behind the barriers. A few metres behind this rope, a second, thinner and shorter one is stretched between the stands and the winch that secures it, allowing just enough room for the horses to get in between the two ropes for the start-off (mossa). A metal cage, containing the «mortaletti» (crackers) let off at various points of the event, as signals, is then hoisted up beside the winch.

The standard of the "Eagle".

Above: the standard of the "Snail".
Below: the standard of the "Owl".

Above: the standard of the "Caterpillar".
Below: the standard of the "Porcupine".

The standard of the "She-wolf".

Above: the standard of the "Giraffe".
Below: the standard of the "Goose".

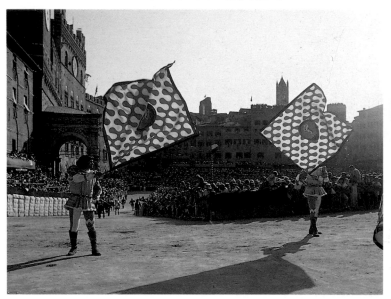

Above: the standard of the "Unicorn".
Below: the standard of the "Dragon".

The standard of the "Shell".

Above: the standard of the "Wave".
Below: the standard of the "Panther".

Above: the standard of the "Forest".
Below: the standard of the "Tower".

Above: the standard of the "Tortoise".
Below: detail of the Palio Cortège.

The standard of the "Ram".

carries the «Balzana» (Sienese Standard), the trumpet players and the Palio: a silken standard painted by famous Italian and non-Italian artists (the July Palio: a Sienese artist – the August Palio: a famous artist from outside Siena). The Palio, is given to the winning Contrada, whereas the Contrada judged the best during the procession, both because of the stateliness of the Comparsa's behaviour, as well as for the ability of the squires in drumming and in handling and «hurling» the standards, will subsequently receive the «masgalano» (a finely chased silver dish). After accompanying their Comparsa to Piazza del Duomo, the People of the contrade take up their positions in piazza del Campo. Once the Historical Cortège has filed around the earth track on the Piazza del Campo, all the costumed representatives of the Contrade take their seats on the great stand set up in front of the Palazzo Pubblico. One drummer and one standard-bearer for each Contrada stay on the tufa-track for the collective standard display, which is the last salute payed to the crowd before the race; in the meantime the Palio is hoisted into position on the Judges' Stand. And the Palio is on: at the signal, the horses – on which the jockeys, wearing the colours of the contrade ride bare-back, with hard metal caps (zucchini) protecting their heads –are led out of the Courtyard of the Podestà. As they emerge, each jockey is given a «nerbo» or crop (made out of an essicated bull's phallus) with which they will be able to urge on their own horse and hit the jockeys and horses of the other contrade. They proceed to the «mossa» (starting post) where a special machine draws lots as to the order in which the horses are to enter the gap between the two ropes. The horse of the last and tenth Contrada drawn is the «runner-up» (di rincorsa) and as soon as this horse enters the gap, the «mossiere» (starter) gives the starting signal which will be repeated if he judges that the

Above: the "Canapo" drops and the horses are off!. *Below*: the horses swerving
around the San Martino bend.

Above: **the arrival of the winner and the exultant joy of the "contradaioli".** *Below*:
the "Victory Banquet" in the "Eagle" Contrada.

horses have got off to a false start. As soon as the rope drops, the horses spurt forward and the jockeys fight each other in every way they can. One of the horses will be the winner, even if he gets to the finish riderless, because it is the horse that gets to the end of the race that wins, not the rider. The deliriously exultant contrada members brandish their banners as the Palio is handed down to them from the judges' stand and chant their way towards the Victory Banquet. And the night will resound to their songs of joy. Torches will burn brightly from the Mangia tower, while the colours of the winning contrada hang triumphantly outside the tri-part mullioned window of the Palace.

The Victorious Contrada Celebrates the Palio

The Contrade who have won the two Palio races of the year, generally organise two great banquets, at a few days distance from each other, in the month of September. The contrada is decked with flags and lights and trestle tables are set up along the streets, for the some 3/4000 hungry participants at the «Victory Banquet». The "Priore" of the Contrada, flanked by the Captain and the victorious jockey will be given the places of honour, together with the Authorities and the specially invited guests. Most important of all, in the centre, opposite the places of honour, a special horse-box with a manger, will be set-up for the «barbero» (steed).

Antonio Zazzeroni

INDEX